Third Workshop on Structured Prediction for NLP 2019

Minneapolis, Minnesota, USA
7 June 2019

ISBN: 978-1-5108-8769-5

Printed from e-media with permission by:

Curran Associates, Inc.
57 Morehouse Lane
Red Hook, NY 12571

Some format issues inherent in the e-media version may also appear in this print version.

Printed by Curran Associates, Inc. (2019)

Association for Computational Linguistics
209 N. Eighth Street
Stroudsburg, Pennsylvania 18360

Phone: 1-570-476-8006
Fax: 1-570-476-0860

acl@aclweb.org

Additional copies of this publication are available from:

Curran Associates, Inc.
57 Morehouse Lane
Red Hook, NY 12571 USA
Phone: 845-758-0400
Fax: 845-758-2633
Email: curran@proceedings.com
Web: www.proceedings.com

NAACL HLT 2019

Structured Prediction for NLP

Proceedings of the Third Workshop

June 7, 2019
Minneapolis, Minnesota, USA

Introduction

Welcome to the Third Workshop on Structured Prediction for NLP!

Structured prediction has a strong tradition within the natural language processing (NLP) community, owing to the discrete, compositional nature of words and sentences, which leads to natural combinatorial representations such as trees, sequences, segments, or alignments, among others. It is no surprise that structured output models have been successful and popular in NLP applications since their inception. Many other NLP tasks, including, but not limited to: semantic parsing, slot filling, machine translation, or information extraction, are commonly modeled as structured problems, and accounting for said structure has often lead to performance gain.

Of late, continuous representation learning via neural networks has been a significant complementary direction, leading to improvements in unsupervised and semi-supervised pre-training, transfer learning, domain adaptation, *etc.* Using word embeddings as features for structured models such as part-of-speech taggers count among the very first uses of continuous embeddings in NLP, and the symbiosis between the two approaches is an exciting research direction today.

The five papers (as well as three additional non-archival papers) accepted for presentation in this edition of the workshop, after double-blind peer review, all explore this interplay between structure and neural data representations, from different, important points of view. The program includes work on structure-informed representation learning, transfer learning, partial supervision, and parallelization of computation in structured computation graphs. Our program also includes six invited presentations from influential researchers.

Our warmest thanks go to the program committee – for their time and effort providing valuable feedback, to all submitting authors – for their thought-provoking work, and to the invited speakers – for doing us the honor of joining our program. We are looking forward to seeing you in Minneapolis!

Zornitsa Kozareva
Julia Kreutzer
Gerasimos Lampouras
André Martins
Vlad Niculae
Sujith Ravi
Andreas Vlachos

Organizers:

Zornitsa Kozareva, Google, USA
Julia Kreutzer, Heidelberg University, Germany
Gerasimos Lampouras, University of Cambridge, UK
André F.T. Martins, Unbabel & University of Lisbon, Portugal
Vlad Niculae, University of Lisbon, Portugal
Sujith Ravi, Google, USA
Andreas Vlachos, University of Cambridge, UK

Program Committee:

Yoav Artzi, Cornell University, USA
Wilker Aziz, University of Amsterdam, Netherlands
Joost Bastings, University of Amsterdam, Netherlands
Xilun Chen, Cornell University, USA
Shay Cohen, University of Edinburgh, UK
Hal Daumé, Microsoft & University of Maryland, USA
Kevin Gimpel, TTI Chicago, USA
Matt Gormley, CMU, USA
Arzoo Katiyar, Cornell University, USA
Yoon Kim, Harvard University, USA
Parisa Kordjamshidi, Tulane University, USA
Amandla Mabona, University of Cambridge, UK
Pranava Madhyastha, Imperial College London, UK
Sebastian Mielke, Johns Hopkins University, USA
Roi Reichart, Technion - Israel Institute of Technology, Israel
Marek Rei, University of Cambridge, UK
Stefan Riezler, Heidelberg University, Germany
Hiko Schamoni, Heidelberg University, Germany
Tianze Shi, Cornell University, USA
Artem Sokolov, Amazon, Germany
Vivek Srikumar, University of Utah, USA
Ivan Titov, University of Edinburgh, Scotland
Luke Zettlemoyer, University of Washington, USA

Invited Speakers:

Claire Cardie, Cornell University, USA
Chris Dyer, DeepMind, UK
Jason Eisner, Johns Hopkins University, USA
Hannaneh Hajishirzi, University of Washington, USA
He He, Stanford University, USA
Andrew McCallum, University of Massachusetts Amherst, USA

Table of Contents

Workshop Program

Friday, June 7, 2019

9:00–9:10 ***Opening Remarks***

9:10–9:50 *Invited Talk: Andrew McCallum*

9:50–10:30 *Invited Talk: Hannaneh Hajishirzi*

10:30–11:00 ***Coffee Break***

11:00–11:40 *Invited Talk by He He*

11:40–12:10 ***Session 1: Contributed Talks***

11:40–11:55 *Parallelizable Stack Long Short-Term Memory*
Shuoyang Ding and Philipp Koehn

11:55–12:10 *Tracking Discrete and Continuous Entity State for Process Understanding*
Aditya Gupta and Greg Durrett

12:10–14:00 ***Lunch***

14:00–14:40 *Invited Talk: Chris Dyer*

14:40–15:00 ***Poster Spotlight***

15:00–16:00 ***Poster Session (and non-archival papers)***

SPARSE: Structured Prediction using Argument-Relative Structured Encoding
Rishi Bommasani, Arzoo Katiyar and Claire Cardie

Friday, June 7, 2019 (continued)

Lightly-supervised Representation Learning with Global Interpretability
Andrew Zupon, Maria Alexeeva, Marco Valenzuela-Escárcega, Ajay Nagesh and Mihai Surdeanu

Semi-Supervised Teacher-Student Architecture for Relation Extraction
Fan Luo, Ajay Nagesh, Rebecca Sharp and Mihai Surdeanu

15:30–16:00 ***Coffee Break (With Posters)***

16:00–16:40 *Invited Talk: Claire Cardie*

16:40–17:20 *Invited Talk: Jason Eisner*

Parallelizable Stack Long Short-Term Memory

Shuoyang Ding Philipp Koehn
Center for Language and Speech Processing
Johns Hopkins University
{dings, phi}@jhu.edu

Abstract

Stack Long Short-Term Memory (StackLSTM) is useful for various applications such as parsing and string-to-tree neural machine translation, but it is also known to be notoriously difficult to parallelize for GPU training due to the fact that the computations are dependent on discrete operations. In this paper, we tackle this problem by utilizing state access patterns of StackLSTM to homogenize computations with regard to different discrete operations. Our parsing experiments show that the method scales up almost linearly with increasing batch size, and our parallelized PyTorch implementation trains significantly faster compared to the Dynet C++ implementation.

1 Introduction

Tree-structured representation of language has been successfully applied to various applications including dependency parsing (Dyer et al., 2015), sentiment analysis (Socher et al., 2011) and neural machine translation (Eriguchi et al., 2017). However, most of the neural network architectures used to build tree-structured representations are not able to exploit full parallelism of GPUs by minibatched training, as the computation that happens for each instance is conditioned on the input/output structures, and hence cannot be naïvely grouped together as a batch. This lack of parallelism is one of the major hurdles that prevent these representations from wider adoption practically (e.g., neural machine translation), as many natural language processing tasks currently require the ability to scale up to very large training corpora in order to reach state-of-the-art performance.

We seek to advance the state-of-the-art of this problem by proposing a parallelization scheme for one such network architecture, the Stack Long Short-Term Memory (StackLSTM) proposed in Dyer et al. (2015). This architecture has been successfully applied to dependency parsing (Dyer et al., 2015, 2016; Ballesteros et al., 2017) and syntax-aware neural machine translation (Eriguchi et al., 2017) in the previous research literature, but none of these research results were produced with minibatched training. We show that our parallelization scheme is feasible in practice by showing that it scales up near-linearly with increasing batch size, while reproducing a set of results reported in (Ballesteros et al., 2017).

2 StackLSTM

StackLSTM (Dyer et al., 2015) is an LSTM architecture (Hochreiter and Schmidhuber, 1997) augmented with a stack $\mathcal{H}$ that stores some of the hidden states built in the past. Unlike traditional LSTMs that always build state h_t from h_{t-1}, the states of StackLSTM are built from the head of the state stack $\mathcal{H}$, maintained by a stack top pointer $p(\mathcal{H})$. At each time step, StackLSTM takes a real-valued input vector together with an additional discrete operation on the stack, which determines what computation needs to be conducted and how the stack top pointer should be updated. Throughout this section, we index the input vector (e.g. word embeddings) x_t using the time step t it is fed into the network, and hidden states in the stack h_j using their position j in the stack $\mathcal{H}$, j being defined as the 0-base index starting from the stack bottom.

The set of input discrete actions typically contains at least `Push` and `Pop` operations. When these operations are taken as input, the corresponding computations on the StackLSTM are listed below:[1]

- `Push`: read previous hidden state $h_{p(\mathcal{H})}$, perform LSTM forward computation with x_t and

[1]To simplify the presentation, we omitted the updates on cell states, because in practice the operations performed on cell states and hidden states are the same.

Proceedings of 3rd Workshop on Structured Prediction for NLP, pages 1–6
Minneapolis, Minnesota, June 7, 2019.

Transition Systems	Transition Op	Stack Op	Buffer Op	Composition Op
Arc-Standard	Shift	push	pop	none
	Left-Arc	pop, pop, push	hold	$S1 \leftarrow g(S0, S1)$
	Right-Arc	pop	hold	$S1 \leftarrow g(S1, S0)$
Arc-Eager	Shift	push	pop	none
	Reduce	pop	hold	none
	Left-Arc	pop	hold	$B0 \leftarrow g(B0, S0)$
	Right-Arc	push	pop	$B0 \leftarrow g(S0, B0)$
Arc-Hybrid	Shift	push	pop	none
	Left-Arc	pop	hold	$B0 \leftarrow g(B0, S0)$
	Right-Arc	pop	hold	$S1 \leftarrow g(S1, S0)$

Table 1: Correspondence between transition operations and stack/buffer operations for StackLSTM, where g denotes the composition function as proposed by (Dyer et al., 2015). S0 and B0 refers to the token-level representation corresponding to the top element of the stack and buffer, while S1 and B1 refers to those that are second to the top. We use a different notation here to avoid confusion with the states in StackLSTM, which represent non-local information beyond token-level.

$h_{p(\mathcal{H})}$, write new hidden state to $h_{p(\mathcal{H})+1}$, update stack top pointer with $p(\mathcal{H}) \leftarrow p(\mathcal{H}) + 1$.

- `Pop`: update stack top pointer with $p(\mathcal{H}) \leftarrow p(\mathcal{H}) - 1$.

Reflecting on the aforementioned discussion on parallelism, one should notice that StackLSTM falls into the category of neural network architectures that is difficult to perform minibatched training. This is caused by the fact that the computation performed by StackLSTM at each time step is dependent on the discrete input actions. The following section proposes a solution to this problem.

3 Parallelizable StackLSTM

Continuing the formulation in the previous section, we will start by discussing our proposed solution under the case where the set of discrete actions contains only `Push` and `Pop` operations; we then move on to discussion of the applicability of our proposed solution to the transition systems that are used for building representations for dependency trees.

The first modification we perform to the `Push` and `Pop` operations above is to unify the pointer update of these operations as $p(\mathcal{H}) \leftarrow p(\mathcal{H}) + op$, where *op* is the input discrete operation that could either take the value +1 or -1 for `Push` and `Pop` operation. After this modification, we came to the following observations:

Observation 1 *The computation performed for* `Pop` *operation is a subset of* `Push` *operation.*

Now, what remains to homogenize `Push` and `Pop` operations is conducting the extra computations needed for `Push` operation when `Pop` is fed in as well, while guaranteeing the correctness of the resulting hidden state both in the current time step and in the future. The next observation points out a way for this guarantee:

Observation 2 *In a StackLSTM, given the current stack top pointer position $p(\mathcal{H})$, any hidden state h_i where $i > p(\mathcal{H})$ will not be read until it is overwritten by a* `Push` *operation.*

What follows from this observation is the guarantee that we can always safely overwrite hidden states h_i that are indexed higher than the current stack top pointer, because it is known that any read operation on these states will happen after another overwrite. This allows us to *do the extra computation anyway* when `Pop` operation is fed, because the extra computation, especially updating $h_{p(\mathcal{H})+1}$, will not harm the validity of the hidden states at any time step.

Algorithm 1 gives the final forward computation for the Parallelizable StackLSTM. Note that this algorithm does not contain any if-statements that depends on stack operations and hence is homogeneous when grouped into batches that are consisted of multiple operations trajectories.

In transition systems (Nivre, 2008; Kuhlmann et al., 2011) used in real tasks (e.g., transition-based parsing) as shown in Table 1, it should be noted that more than `push` and `pop` operations are needed for the StackLSTM. Fortunately, for Arc-Eager and

Algorithm 1: Forward Computation for Parallelizable StackLSTM

Input: input vector x_t
discrete stack operation op
Output: current top hidden state $h_{p(\mathcal{H})}$
$h\_prev \leftarrow h_{p(\mathcal{H})}$;
$h \leftarrow \text{LSTM}(x_t, h\_prev)$;
$h_{p(\mathcal{H})+1} \leftarrow h$;
$p(\mathcal{H}) \leftarrow p(\mathcal{H}) + op$;
return $h_{p(\mathcal{H})}$;

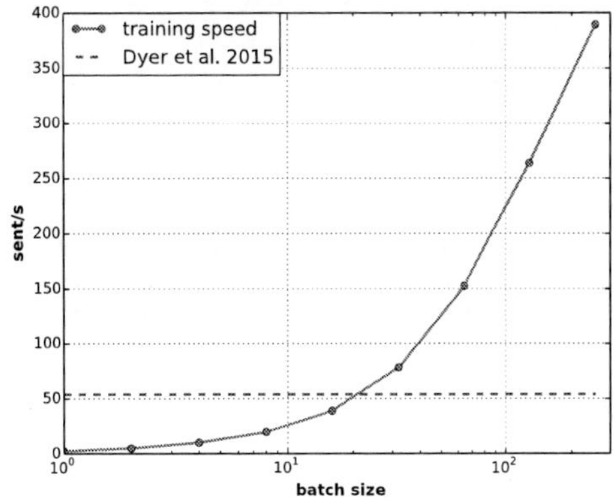

Figure 1: Training speed at different batch size. Note that the x-axis is in log-scale in order to show all the data points properly.

Arc-Hybrid transition systems, we can simply add a `hold` operation, which is denoted by value 0 for the discrete operation input. For that reason, we will focus on parallelization of these two transition systems for this paper. It should be noted that both observations discussed above are still valid after adding the `hold` operation.

4 Experiments

4.1 Setup

We implemented[2] the architecture described above in PyTorch (Paszke et al., 2017). We implemented the batched stack as a float tensor wrapped in a non-leaf variable, thus enabling in-place operations on that variable. At each time step, the batched stack is queried/updated with a batch of stack head positions represented by an integer vector, an operation made possible by `gather` operation and advanced indexing. Due to this implementation choice, the stack size has to be determined at initialization time and cannot be dynamically grown. Nonetheless, a fixed stack size of 150 works for all the experiments we conducted.

We use the dependency parsing task to evaluate the correctness and the scalability of our method. For comparison with previous work, we follow the architecture introduced in Dyer et al. (2015); Ballesteros et al. (2017) and chose the Arc-Hybrid transition system for comparison with previous work. We follow the data setup in Chen and Manning (2014); Dyer et al. (2015); Ballesteros et al. (2017) and use Stanford Dependency Treebank (de Marneffe et al., 2006) for dependency parsing, and we extract the Arc-Hybrid static oracle using the code associated with Qi and Manning (2017). The part-of-speech (POS) tags are generated with Stanford POS-tagger (Toutanova et al., 2003) with a test set accuracy of 97.47%. We use exactly the same pre-trained English word embedding as Dyer et al. (2015).

We use Adam (Kingma and Ba, 2014) as the optimization algorithm. Following Goyal et al. (2017), we apply linear warmup to the learning rate with an initial value of $\tau = 5 \times 10^{-4}$ and total epoch number of 5. The target learning rate is set by τ multiplied by batch size, but capped at 0.02 because we find Adam to be unstable beyond that learning rate. After warmup, we reduce the learning rate by half every time there is no improvement for loss value on the development set (`ReduceLROnPlateau`). We clip all the gradient norms to 5.0 and apply a L_2-regularization with weight 1×10^{-6}.

We started with the hyper-parameter choices in Dyer et al. (2015) but made some modifications based on the performance on the development set: we use hidden dimension 200 for all the LSTM units, 200 for the parser state representation before the final softmax layer, and embedding dimension 48 for the action embedding.

We use Tesla K80 for all the experiments, in order to compare with Neubig et al. (2017b); Dyer et al. (2015). We also use the same hyper-parameter setting as Dyer et al. (2015) for speed comparison experiments. All the speeds are measured by running through one training epoch and averaging.

4.2 Results

Figure 1 shows the training speed at different batch sizes up to 256.[3] The speed-up of our model is

[2] https://github.com/shuoyangd/hoolock

[3] At batch size of 512, the longest sentence in the training data cannot be fit onto the GPU.

b	dev		test	
	UAS	LAS	UAS	LAS
1*	92.50*	89.79*	92.10*	89.61*
8	92.93	90.42	92.54	90.11
16	92.62	90.19	92.53	90.13
32	92.43	89.89	92.31	89.94
64	92.53	90.04	92.22	89.73
128	92.39	89.73	92.55	90.02
256	92.15	89.46	91.99	89.43

Table 2: Dependency parsing result with various training batch size b and without composition function. The results marked with asterisks were reported in the Ballesteros et al. (2017).

close to linear, which means there is very little overhead associated with our batching scheme. Quantitatively, according to Amdahl's Law (Amdahl, 1967), the proportion of parallelized computations is 99.92% at batch size 64. We also compared our implementation with the implementation that comes with Dyer et al. (2015), which is implemented in C++ with DyNet (Neubig et al., 2017a). DyNet is known to be very optimized for CPU computations and hence their implementation is reasonably fast even without batching and GPU acceleration, as shown in Figure 1.[4] But we would like to point out that we focus on the speed-up we are able to obtain rather than the absolute speed, and that our batching scheme is framework-universal and superior speed might be obtained by combining our scheme with alternative frameworks or languages (for example, the torch C++ interface).

The dependency parsing results are shown in Table 2. Our implementation is able to yield better test set performance than that reported in Ballesteros et al. (2017) for all batch size configurations except 256, where we observe a modest performance loss. Like Goyal et al. (2017); Keskar et al. (2016); Masters and Luschi (2018), we initially observed more significant test-time performance deterioration (around 1% absolute difference) for models trained without learning rate warmup, and concurring with the findings in Goyal et al. (2017), we find warmup very helpful for stabilizing large-batch training. We did not run experiments with batch size below 8 as they are too slow due to Python's inherent performance issue.

5 Related Work

DyNet has support for automatic minibatching (Neubig et al., 2017b), which figures out what computation is able to be batched by traversing the computation graph to find homogeneous computations. While we cannot directly compare with that framework's automatic batching solution for StackLSTM[5], we can draw a loose comparison to the results reported in that paper for BiLSTM transition-based parsing (Kiperwasser and Goldberg, 2016). Comparing batch size of 64 to batch size of 1, they obtained a 3.64x speed-up on CPU and 2.73x speed-up on Tesla K80 GPU, while our architecture-specific manual batching scheme obtained 60.8x speed-up. The main reason for this difference is that their graph-traversing automatic batching scheme carries a much larger overhead compared to our manual batching approach.

Another toolkit that supports automatic minibatching is Matchbox[6], which operates by analyzing the single-instance model definition and deterministically convert the operations into their minibatched counterparts. While such mechanism eliminated the need to traverse the whole computation graph, it cannot homogenize the operations in each branch of `if`. Instead, it needs to perform each operation separately and apply masking on the result, while our method does not require any masking. Unfortunately we are also not able to compare with the toolkit at the time of this work as it lacks support for several operations we need.

Similar to the spirit of our work, Bowman et al. (2016) attempted to parallelize StackLSTM by using *Thin-stack*, a data structure that reduces the space complexity by storing all the intermediate stack top elements in a tensor and use a queue to control element access. However, thanks to PyTorch, our implementation is not directly dependent on the notion of Thin-stack. Instead, when an element is popped from the stack, we simply shift the stack top pointer and potentially re-write the corresponding sub-tensor later. In other words, there is no need for us to directly maintain all the intermediate stack top elements, because in PyTorch, when the element in the stack is re-written, its underlying sub-tensor will not be destructed as there

[4]Measured on one core of an Intel Xeon E7-4830 CPU.

[5]This is due to the fact that DyNet automatic batching cannot handle graph structures that depends on runtime input values, which is the case in StackLSTM.

[6]`https://github.com/salesforce/matchbox`

are still nodes in the computation graph that point to it. Hence, when performing back-propagation, the gradient is still able to flow back to the elements that are previously popped from the stack and their respective precedents. Hence, we are also effectively storing all the intermediate stack top elements only once. Besides, Bowman et al. (2016) didn't attempt to eliminate the conditional branches in the StackLSTM algorithm, which is the main algorithmic contribution of this work.

6 Conclusion

We propose a parallelizable version of StackLSTM that is able to fully exploit the GPU parallelism by performing minibatched training. Empirical results show that our parallelization scheme yields comparable performance to previous work, and our method scales up very linearly with the increasing batch size.

Because our parallelization scheme is based on the observation made in section 1, we cannot incorporate batching for neither Arc-Standard transition system nor the token-level composition function proposed in Dyer et al. (2015) efficiently yet. We leave the parallelization of these architectures to future work.

Our parallelization scheme makes it feasible to run large-data experiments for various tasks that requires large training data to perform well, such as RNNG-based syntax-aware neural machine translation (Eriguchi et al., 2017).

Acknowledgement

The authors would like to thank Peng Qi for helping with data preprocessing and James Bradbury for helpful technical discussions. This material is based upon work supported in part by the DARPA LORELEI and IARPA MATERIAL programs.

References

Gene M. Amdahl. 1967. Validity of the single processor approach to achieving large scale computing capabilities. In *American Federation of Information Processing Societies: Proceedings of the AFIPS '67 Spring Joint Computer Conference, April 18-20, 1967, Atlantic City, New Jersey, USA*, pages 483–485.

Miguel Ballesteros, Chris Dyer, Yoav Goldberg, and Noah A. Smith. 2017. Greedy transition-based dependency parsing with stack lstms. *Computational Linguistics*, 43(2):311–347.

Samuel R. Bowman, Jon Gauthier, Abhinav Rastogi, Raghav Gupta, Christopher D. Manning, and Christopher Potts. 2016. A fast unified model for parsing and sentence understanding. In *Proceedings of the 54th Annual Meeting of the Association for Computational Linguistics, ACL 2016, August 7-12, 2016, Berlin, Germany, Volume 1: Long Papers*.

Danqi Chen and Christopher D. Manning. 2014. A fast and accurate dependency parser using neural networks. In *Proceedings of the 2014 Conference on Empirical Methods in Natural Language Processing, EMNLP 2014, October 25-29, 2014, Doha, Qatar, A meeting of SIGDAT, a Special Interest Group of the ACL*, pages 740–750.

Chris Dyer, Miguel Ballesteros, Wang Ling, Austin Matthews, and Noah A. Smith. 2015. Transition-based dependency parsing with stack long short-term memory. In *Proceedings of the 53rd Annual Meeting of the Association for Computational Linguistics and the 7th International Joint Conference on Natural Language Processing of the Asian Federation of Natural Language Processing, ACL 2015, July 26-31, 2015, Beijing, China, Volume 1: Long Papers*, pages 334–343.

Chris Dyer, Adhiguna Kuncoro, Miguel Ballesteros, and Noah A. Smith. 2016. Recurrent neural network grammars. In *NAACL HLT 2016, The 2016 Conference of the North American Chapter of the Association for Computational Linguistics: Human Language Technologies, San Diego California, USA, June 12-17, 2016*, pages 199–209.

Akiko Eriguchi, Yoshimasa Tsuruoka, and Kyunghyun Cho. 2017. Learning to parse and translate improves neural machine translation. In *Proceedings of the 55th Annual Meeting of the Association for Computational Linguistics, ACL 2017, Vancouver, Canada, July 30 - August 4, Volume 2: Short Papers*, pages 72–78.

Priya Goyal, Piotr Dollár, Ross B. Girshick, Pieter Noordhuis, Lukasz Wesolowski, Aapo Kyrola, Andrew Tulloch, Yangqing Jia, and Kaiming He. 2017. Accurate, large minibatch SGD: training imagenet in 1 hour. *CoRR*, abs/1706.02677.

Sepp Hochreiter and Jürgen Schmidhuber. 1997. Long short-term memory. *Neural Computation*, 9(8):1735–1780.

Nitish Shirish Keskar, Dheevatsa Mudigere, Jorge Nocedal, Mikhail Smelyanskiy, and Ping Tak Peter Tang. 2016. On large-batch training for deep learning: Generalization gap and sharp minima. *CoRR*, abs/1609.04836.

Diederik P. Kingma and Jimmy Ba. 2014. Adam: A method for stochastic optimization. *CoRR*, abs/1412.6980.

Eliyahu Kiperwasser and Yoav Goldberg. 2016. Simple and accurate dependency parsing using bidirectional LSTM feature representations. *CoRR*, abs/1603.04351.

Marco Kuhlmann, Carlos Gómez-Rodríguez, and Giorgio Satta. 2011. Dynamic programming algorithms for transition-based dependency parsers. In *The 49th Annual Meeting of the Association for Computational Linguistics: Human Language Technologies, Proceedings of the Conference, 19-24 June, 2011, Portland, Oregon, USA*, pages 673–682.

Marie-Catherine de Marneffe, Bill MacCartney, and Christopher D. Manning. 2006. Generating typed dependency parses from phrase structure parses. In *Proceedings of the Fifth International Conference on Language Resources and Evaluation, LREC 2006, Genoa, Italy, May 22-28, 2006.*, pages 449–454.

Dominic Masters and Carlo Luschi. 2018. Revisiting small batch training for deep neural networks. *CoRR*, abs/1804.07612.

Graham Neubig, Chris Dyer, Yoav Goldberg, Austin Matthews, Waleed Ammar, Antonios Anastasopoulos, Miguel Ballesteros, David Chiang, Daniel Clothiaux, Trevor Cohn, Kevin Duh, Manaal Faruqui, Cynthia Gan, Dan Garrette, Yangfeng Ji, Lingpeng Kong, Adhiguna Kuncoro, Gaurav Kumar, Chaitanya Malaviya, Paul Michel, Yusuke Oda, Matthew Richardson, Naomi Saphra, Swabha Swayamdipta, and Pengcheng Yin. 2017a. Dynet: The dynamic neural network toolkit. *CoRR*, abs/1701.03980.

Graham Neubig, Yoav Goldberg, and Chris Dyer. 2017b. On-the-fly operation batching in dynamic computation graphs. In *Advances in Neural Information Processing Systems 30: Annual Conference on Neural Information Processing Systems 2017, 4-9 December 2017, Long Beach, CA, USA*, pages 3974–3984.

Joakim Nivre. 2008. Algorithms for deterministic incremental dependency parsing. *Computational Linguistics*, 34(4):513–553.

Adam Paszke, Sam Gross, Soumith Chintala, Gregory Chanan, Edward Yang, Zachary DeVito, Zeming Lin, Alban Desmaison, Luca Antiga, and Adam Lerer. 2017. Automatic differentiation in pytorch. In *NIPS-W*.

Peng Qi and Christopher D. Manning. 2017. Arc-swift: A novel transition system for dependency parsing. In *Proceedings of the 55th Annual Meeting of the Association for Computational Linguistics, ACL 2017, Vancouver, Canada, July 30 - August 4, Volume 2: Short Papers*, pages 110–117.

Richard Socher, Cliff Chiung-Yu Lin, Andrew Y. Ng, and Christopher D. Manning. 2011. Parsing natural scenes and natural language with recursive neural networks. In *Proceedings of the 28th International Conference on Machine Learning, ICML 2011, Bellevue, Washington, USA, June 28 - July 2, 2011*, pages 129–136.

Kristina Toutanova, Dan Klein, Christopher D. Manning, and Yoram Singer. 2003. Feature-rich part-of-speech tagging with a cyclic dependency network. In *Human Language Technology Conference of the North American Chapter of the Association for Computational Linguistics, HLT-NAACL 2003, Edmonton, Canada, May 27 - June 1, 2003*.

Tracking Discrete and Continuous Entity State for Process Understanding

Aditya Gupta and **Greg Durrett**
Department of Computer Science
The University of Texas at Austin
{agupta,gdurrett}@cs.utexas.edu

Abstract

Procedural text, which describes entities and their interactions as they undergo some process, depicts entities in a uniquely nuanced way. First, each entity may have some observable discrete attributes, such as its state or location; modeling these involves imposing global structure and enforcing consistency. Second, an entity may have properties which are not made explicit but can be effectively induced and tracked by neural networks. In this paper, we propose a structured neural architecture that reflects this dual nature of entity evolution. The model tracks each entity recurrently, updating its hidden continuous representation at each step to contain relevant state information. The global discrete state structure is explicitly modelled with a neural CRF over the changing hidden representation of the entity. This CRF can explicitly capture constraints on entity states over time, enforcing that, for example, an entity cannot move to a location after it is destroyed. We evaluate the performance of our proposed model on QA tasks over process paragraphs in the PROPARA dataset (Dalvi et al., 2018) and find that our model achieves state-of-the-art results.

1 Introduction

Many reading comprehension question answering tasks (Richardson et al., 2013; Rajpurkar et al., 2016; Joshi et al., 2017) require looking at primarily one point in the passage to answer each question, or sometimes two or three (Yang et al., 2018; Welbl et al., 2018). As a result, modeling surface-level correspondences can work well (Seo et al., 2017) and holistic passage comprehension is not necessary. However, certain QA settings require deeper analysis by focusing specifically on entities, asking questions about their states over time (Weston et al., 2015; Long et al., 2016), combination in recipes (Bosselut et al., 2018), and participation in scientific processes (Dalvi et al., 2018). These settings then suggest more highly structured models as a way of dealing with the more highly structured tasks. One crucial aspect of such texts is the way an entity's state evolves with both discrete (observable state and location changes) and continuous (changes in unobserved hidden attributes) phenomena going on. Additionally, the discrete changes unfold in a way that maintains the state consistency: an entity can not be *destroyed* before it even starts to *exist*.

In this work, we present a model which both recurrently tracks the entity in a continuous space while imposing discrete constraints using a conditional random field (CRF). We focus on the scientific process understanding setting introduced in Dalvi et al. (2018). For each entity, we instantiate a sentence-level LSTM to distill continuous state information from each of that entity's mentions. Separate LSTMs integrate entity-location information into this process. These continuous components then produce potentials for a sequential CRF tagging layer, which predicts discrete entity states. The CRF's problem-specific tag scheme, along with transition constraints, ensures that the model's predictions of these observed entity properties are structurally coherent. For example, in procedural texts, this involves ensuring existence before destruction and unique creation and destruction points. Because we use global inference, identifying implicit event creation or destruction is made easier, since the model resolves conflicts among competing time steps and chooses the best time step for these events during sequence prediction.

Past approaches in the literature have typically been end-to-end continuous task specific frameworks (Henaff et al., 2017; Bosselut et al., 2018), sometimes for tasks that are simpler and more syn-

Proceedings of 3rd Workshop on Structured Prediction for NLP, pages 7–12
Minneapolis, Minnesota, June 7, 2019.

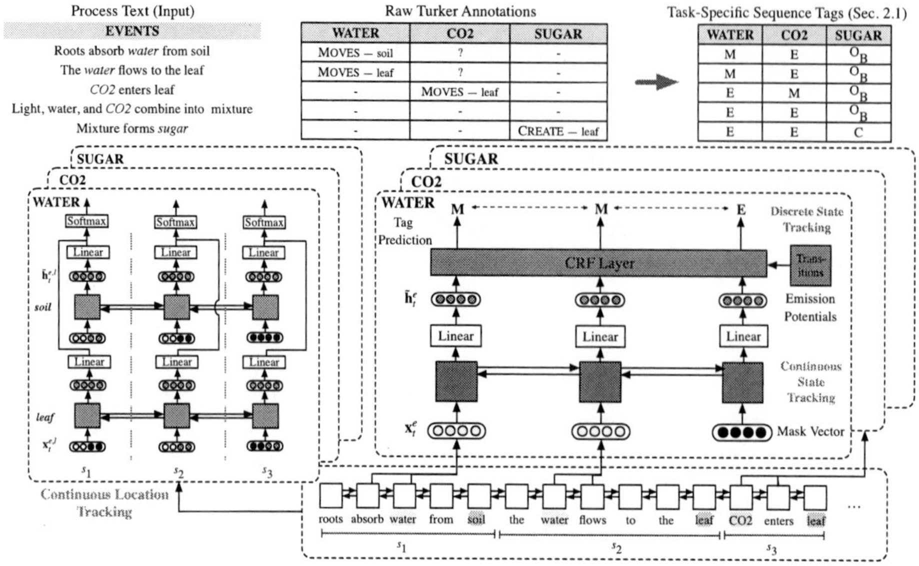

Figure 1: Task and our proposed model. Top: raw text descriptions are annotated with entity-state change information; we modify this in a rule-based way for our model. Bottom: our model. Entity mention and verb information is aggregated in per-entity LSTMs (right). A CRF layer then predicts entity state. A separate sentence-level LSTM (left) tracks each entity-location pair using the combined entity and location mention information.

thetic (Weston et al., 2015), or continuous entity-centric neural language models (Clark et al., 2018; Ji et al., 2017). For process understanding specifically, past work has effectively captured global information (Dalvi et al., 2018) and temporal characteristics (Das et al., 2019). However, these models do not leverage the structure constraints of the problem, or only handle them heuristically (Tandon et al., 2018). We find that our model outperforms these past approaches on the ProPara dataset of Dalvi et al. (2018) with a significant boost in questions concerning entity state, regardless of the location.

2 Model

We propose a structured neural model for the process paragraph comprehension task of Dalvi et al. (2018). An example from their dataset is shown in Figure 1. It consists of annotation over a process paragraph $\mathbf{w} = \{w_i\}_{i=1}^{P}$ of P tokens described by a sequence of T sentences $\mathbf{s} = \{\mathbf{s}_t\}_{t=1}^{T}$. A pre-specified set of entities $E = \{e_k\}_{k=1}^{m}$ is given as well. For each entity, gold annotation is provided consisting of the state (Exists, Moves, etc.) and location (*soil, leaf*) after each sentence. From this information, a set of questions about the process can be answered deterministically as outlined in Tandon et al. (2018).

Our model, as depicted in Fig. 1, consists of two core modules: (i) state tracking, and (ii) location tracking. We follow past work on neural CRFs (Collobert et al., 2011; Durrett and Klein, 2015; Lample et al., 2016), leveraging continuous LSTMs to distill information and a discrete CRF layer for prediction.

2.1 State Tracking

This part of the model is charged with modeling each entity's state over time. Our model places a distribution over state sequences $\mathbf{y}$ given a passage $\mathbf{w}$ and an entity e: $P(\mathbf{y}|\mathbf{w}, e)$.

Contextual Embeddings Our model first computes contextual embeddings for each word in the paragraph using a single layered bidirectional LSTM. Each token word w_i is encoded as a vector $\mathbf{x}_i = [emb(w_i); v_i]$ which serves as input to the LSTM. Here, $emb(w_i) \in \mathbb{R}^{d_1}$ is an embedding for the word produced by either pre-trained GloVe (Pennington et al., 2014) or ELMo (Peters et al., 2018) embeddings and v_i is a scalar binary indicator if the current word is a verb. We denote by $\mathbf{h}_i = \text{LSTM}([\mathbf{x}_i])$ the LSTM's output for the ith token in $\mathbf{w}$.

Entity Tracking LSTM To track entities across sentences for state changes, we use another task specific bidirectional LSTM on top of the base LSTM which operates at the sentence level. The aim of this BiLSTM is to get a continuous representation of the entity's state at each time step, since not all time steps mention that entity. This representation can capture long-range information about the entity's state which may not be summarized in the discrete representation.

For a fixed entity e and each sentence $\mathbf{s}_t$ in the paragraph, the input to the entity tracking LSTM is the contextual embedding of the *mention location*[1] of the entity e in $\mathbf{s}_t$, or a mask vector when the entity isn't present in $\mathbf{s}_t$. Let $\mathbf{x}_t^e$ denote the representation of entity e in sentence t. Then

$$\mathbf{x}_t^e = \begin{cases} [\mathbf{h}_t^e; \mathbf{h}_t^v], & \text{if } e \in \mathbf{s}_t \\ \text{zero vector}, & \text{otherwise} \end{cases} \quad (1)$$

where $\mathbf{h}_t^e$ and $\mathbf{h}_t^v$ denote the contextual embeddings of the entity and the associated verb, respectively, from the base BiLSTM. In case of multiple tokens, a mean pooling over the token representations is used. Here, the information about verb is extracted using POS tags from an off-the-shelf POS tagger. The entity tracking LSTM then produces representations $\widetilde{\mathbf{h}}_t^e = \text{LSTM}([\mathbf{x}_t^e])$.

Neural CRF We use the output of the entity tracking BiLSTM to generate emission potentials for each tag in our possible tag set at each time step t:

$$\phi(y_t, t, \mathbf{w}, e) = \mathbf{W}_{y_t}^T \widetilde{\mathbf{h}}_t^e \quad (2)$$

where $\mathbf{W}$ is a learnable parameter matrix. For the specific case of entity tracking, we propose a 6 tag scheme where the tags are as follows:

Tags	Description
O_B, O_A	None state before and after existence, resp.
C, D	Creation and destruction event for entity, resp.
E	Exists in the process without any state change
M	Entity moves from loc_a to loc_b

Table 1: Proposed tag scheme for the neural CRF based model for entity tracking.

Additionally, we train a transition matrix to get transition potentials between tags which we denote by $\psi(y_{i-1}, y_i)$ and two extra tags: $\langle \mathbf{START} \rangle$ and $\langle \mathbf{STOP} \rangle$. Finally, for a tag sequence $\mathbf{y}$, we get the probability as:

$$P(\mathbf{y}|\mathbf{w}, e) \propto \exp\Big(\sum_{i=0}^{T} \phi_i(y_i, \mathbf{w}, e) + \psi(y_{i-1}, y_i)\Big) \quad (3)$$

2.2 Location Tracking

To complement entity's state changes with the change in physical location of the entity, we use a separate recurrent module to predict the locations. Given a set of potential locations $L = (l_1, l_2, \ldots, l_n)$, where each $l_j \in L$ is a continuous span in $\mathbf{w}$, the location predictor outputs a distribution for a passage $\mathbf{w}$ and entity e, at a given time step t as $P(l|\mathbf{w}, e, t)$.

Identifying potential locations Instead of considering all the spans of text as candidates for potential locations, we systematically reduce the set of locations by utilizing the part of speech (POS) tags of the tokens, whereby extracting all the maximal *noun* and *noun + adjective* spans as potential *physical* location spans. Thus, using an off-the-shelf POS tagger, we get a set $L = (l_1, l_2, \ldots, l_n)$ of potential locations for each $\mathbf{w}$. These heuristics lead to a 85% recall classifier for locations which are not null or unk.[2]

Location Tracking LSTM For a given location l and an entity e, we take the mean of the hidden representations of tokens in the span of l in $\mathbf{s}_t$ (or else a mask vector) analogous to the input for entity state tracking LSTM, concatenating it with the mention location of the entity e in $\mathbf{s}_t$, as input for time-step t for the tracking this entity-location pair with $\widetilde{\mathbf{h}}_t^{e,l} = \text{LSTM}\left([\mathbf{x}_t^{e,l}]\right)$. Fig. 1 shows an example where we instantiate location tracking LSTMs for each pair of entity e and potential location l. In the example, $e \in \{water, CO2, sugar\}$ and $l \in \{soil, leaf\}$.

Softmax over Location Potentials The output of the location tracking LSTM is then used to generate potentials by for each entity e and location l pair for a time step t. Taking softmax over the potentials gives us a probability distribution over the locations l at that time step t for that entity e: $p_t^{e,l} = \text{softmax}(\mathbf{w}_{loc}^T \widetilde{\mathbf{h}}_t^{e,l})$

[1] We use *mention* location to differentiate these from the physical entity locations present in this QA domain.

[2] Major non-matching cases include long phrases like "deep in the earth", "side of the fault line", and "area of high elevation" where the heuristics picks "earth", "fault line", and "area", respectively.

Model	Task-1					Task-2		
	Cat-1	**Cat-2**	**Cat-3**	**Macro-Avg**	**Micro-Avg**	**Precision**	**Recall**	F_1
EntNet (Henaff et al., 2017)	51.62	18.83	7.77	26.07	25.96	50.2	33.5	40.2
QRN (Seo et al., 2017)	52.37	15.51	10.92	26.26	26.49	55.5	31.3	40.0
ProGlobal (Dalvi et al., 2018)	62.95	36.39	35.90	45.08	45.37	46.7	52.4	49.4
ProStruct (Tandon et al., 2018)	-	-	-	-	-	74.2	42.1	53.75
KG-MRC (Das et al., 2019)	62.86	40.00	38.23	47.03	46.62	64.52	50.68	56.77
This work: NCET	70.55	44.57	41.34	52.15	52.31	64.2	53.9	58.6
This work: NCET + ELMo	73.68	47.09	41.03	53.93	53.97	67.1	58.5	62.5

Table 2: Results on the sentence-level (Task-1) and document-level (Task-2) evaluation task of the PROPARA dataset on the test set. Our proposed CRF-based model achieves state of the art results on both the tasks compared to the previous work in (Das et al., 2019). Incorporating ELMo further improves the performance for the state tracking module, as we see from the gains in Cat-1 and Cat-2.

2.3 Learning and Inference

The full model is trained end-to-end by minimizing the negative log likelihood of the gold state tag sequence for each entity and process paragraph pair. The location predictor is only trained to make predictions when the gold location is defined for that entity in the dataset (i.e., the entity exists).

At inference time, we perform a global state change inference coupled with location prediction in a pipelined fashion. First, we use the state tracking module of the proposed model to predict the state change sequence with the maximum score using Viterbi decoding. Subsequently, we predict locations where the predicted tag is either *create* or *move*, which is sufficient to identify the object's location at all times since these are the only points where it can change.

3 Experiments

We evaluate the performance of the proposed model on the two comprehension tasks of the PROPARA dataset (Dalvi et al., 2018). This dataset consists of 488 crowdsourced real world process paragraphs about 183 distinct topics in the science genre. The names of the participating entities and their existence spans are identified by expert annotators. Finally, crowd workers label locations of participant entities at each time step (sentence). The final data consists of 3.3k sentence with an average of 6.7 sentences and 4.17 entities per process paragraph. We compare our model, the Neural CRF Entity Tracking (NCET) model, with benchmark systems from past work.

3.1 Task 1: Sentence Level

This comprehension task concerns answering 10 fine grained sentence level templated questions grouped into three categories: **(Cat-1)** Is e Created (Moved, Destroyed) in the process (yes/no for each)? **(Cat-2)** When was e Created (Moved, Destroyed)? **(Cat-3)** Where was e Created, (Moved from/to, Destroyed)? The ground truth for these questions were extracted by the application of simple rules to the annotated location state data. Note that Cat-1 and Cat-2 can be answered from our state-tracking model alone, and only Cat-3 involves location.

As shown in Table 2, our model using GloVe achieves state of the art performance on the test set. The performance gain is attributed to the gains in Cat-1 and Cat-2 (7.69% and 4.57% absolute), owing to the structural constraints imposed by the CRF layer. The gain in Cat-3 is relatively lower as it is the only sub-task involving location tracking. Additionally, using the frozen ELMo embedding the performance further improves with major improvements in Cat-1 and Cat-2.

3.2 Task 2: Document Level

The document level evaluation tries to capture a more global context where the templated[3] questions set forth concern about the whole paragraph structure: (i) What are the inputs to the process? (ii) What are the outputs of the process? (iii) What conversions occur, when and where? (iv) What movements occur, when and where? Table 2 shows the performance of the model on this task. We achieve state of the art results with a F_1 of 58.6.

[3]Inputs refer to the entities which existed prior to the process and are destroyed during it. Outputs refer to the entities which get created in the process without subsequent destruction. Conversion refers to the simultaneous event which involves creation of some entities coupled with destruction of others.

Model	C-1	C-2	C-3	Mac.	Mic.
NCET	72.27	46.08	40.82	53.06	53.13
Tag Set 1	71.53	41.89	41.42	51.61	51.94
Tag Set 2	71.97	41.85	39.71	51.18	51.43
No trans.	71.68	44.22	40.38	52.09	52.24
No verb	73.16	42.58	41.85	52.53	52.85
Attn.	61.69	22.80	36.44	40.31	41.38

Table 3: Ablation studies for the proposed architecture.

3.3 Model Ablations

We now examine the performance of the model by comparing its variants along two different dimensions: (i) modifying the structural constraints for the CRF layer, and (ii) making changes to the continuous entity tracking.

Discrete Structural Constraints We experiment with two new tag schemes: (i) $tag_1 : O_A = O_B$, and (ii) $tag_2 : O_A = E = O_B$. As shown in Table 3, the proposed 6 tag scheme outperforms the simpler tag schemes indicating that the model is able to gain more from a better structural annotation. Additionally, we experiment with removing the transition features from our CRF layer, though we still use structural constraints. Taken together, these results show that carefully capturing the domain constraints in how entities change over time is an important factor in our model.

Continuous Entity Tracking To evaluate the importance of different modules in our continuous entity tracking model, we experiment with (i) removing the verb information, and (ii) taking attention-based input for the entity tracking LSTM instead of the entity-mention information. This way instead of giving a hard attention by focusing exactly on the entity, we let the model learn soft attention across the tokens for each time-step. The model can now learn to look anywhere in a sentence for entity information, but is not given prior knowledge of how to do so. As shown, using attention-based input for entity tracking performs substantially worse, indicating the structural importance of passing the mask vector.

4 Conclusion

In this paper, we present a structured architecture for entity tracking which leverages both the discrete and continuous characterization of the entity evolution. We use a neural CRF approach to model our discrete constraints while tracking entities and locations recurrently. Our model achieves state of the art results on the PROPARA dataset.

Acknowledgments

This work was partially supported by NSF Grant IIS-1814522, NSF Grant SHF-1762299, a Bloomberg Data Science Grant, and an equipment grant from NVIDIA. The authors acknowledge the Texas Advanced Computing Center (TACC) at The University of Texas at Austin for providing HPC resources used to conduct this research. Thanks to the anonymous reviewers for their helpful comments.

References

Antoine Bosselut, Corin Ennis, Omer Levy, Ari Holtzman, Dieter Fox, and Yejin Choi. 2018. Simulating Action Dynamics with Neural Process Networks. In *Proceedings of the International Conference on Learning Representations (ICLR)*.

Elizabeth Clark, Yangfeng Ji, and Noah A. Smith. 2018. Neural Text Generation in Stories Using Entity Representations as Context. In *Proceedings of the 2018 Conference of the North American Chapter of the Association for Computational Linguistics (ACL): Human Language Technologies*.

Ronan Collobert, Jason Weston, Léon Bottou, Michael Karlen, Koray Kavukcuoglu, and Pavel Kuksa. 2011. Natural Language Processing (Almost) from Scratch. *Journal of Machine Learning Research*, 12(Aug):2493–2537.

Bhavana Dalvi, Lifu Huang, Niket Tandon, Wen-tau Yih, and Peter Clark. 2018. Tracking State Changes in Procedural Text: a Challenge Dataset and Models for Process Paragraph Comprehension. In *Proceedings of the Conference of the North American Chapter of the Association for Computational Linguistics (NAACL): Human Language Technologies*.

Rajarshi Das, Tsendsuren Munkhdalai, Xingdi Yuan, Adam Trischler, and Andrew McCallum. 2019. Building Dynamic Knowledge Graphs from Text using Machine Reading Comprehension. In *Proceedings of the International Conference on Learning Representations (ICLR)*.

Greg Durrett and Dan Klein. 2015. Neural CRF Parsing. In *Proceedings of the 53rd Annual Meeting of the Association for Computational Linguistics (ACL) and the 7th International Joint Conference on Natural Language Processing*.

Mikael Henaff, Jason Weston, Arthur Szlam, Antoine Bordes, and Yann LeCun. 2017. Tracking the World

State with Recurrent Entity Networks. In *Proceedings of the International Conference on Learning Representations (ICLR)*.

Yangfeng Ji, Chenhao Tan, Sebastian Martschat, Yejin Choi, and Noah A. Smith. 2017. Dynamic Entity Representations in Neural Language Models. In *Proceedings of the 2017 Conference on Empirical Methods in Natural Language Processing*.

Mandar Joshi, Eunsol Choi, Daniel Weld, and Luke Zettlemoyer. 2017. TriviaQA: A Large Scale Distantly Supervised Challenge Dataset for Reading Comprehension. In *Proceedings of the 55th Annual Meeting of the Association for Computational Linguistics (ACL)*.

Guillaume Lample, Miguel Ballesteros, Sandeep Subramanian, Kazuya Kawakami, and Chris Dyer. 2016. Neural Architectures for Named Entity Recognition. In *Proceedings of the Conference of the North American Chapter of the Association for Computational Linguistics (NAACL): Human Language Technologies*.

Reginald Long, Panupong Pasupat, and Percy Liang. 2016. Simpler Context-Dependent Logical Forms via Model Projections. In *Proceedings of the 54th Annual Meeting of the Association for Computational Linguistics (ACL)*.

Jeffrey Pennington, Richard Socher, and Christopher Manning. 2014. GloVe: Global Vectors for Word Representation. In *Proceedings of the Conference on Empirical Methods in Natural Language Processing (EMNLP)*.

Matthew Peters, Mark Neumann, Mohit Iyyer, Matt Gardner, Christopher Clark, Kenton Lee, and Luke Zettlemoyer. 2018. Deep Contextualized Word Representations. In *Proceedings of the Conference of the North American Chapter of the Association for Computational Linguistics (NAACL): Human Language Technologies*.

Pranav Rajpurkar, Jian Zhang, Konstantin Lopyrev, and Percy Liang. 2016. SQuAD: 100,000+ Questions for Machine Comprehension of Text. In *Proceedings of the Conference on Empirical Methods in Natural Language Processing (EMNLP)*.

Matthew Richardson, Christopher J.C. Burges, and Erin Renshaw. 2013. MCTest: A Challenge Dataset for the Open-Domain Machine Comprehension of Text. In *Proceedings of the Conference on Empirical Methods in Natural Language Processing (EMNLP)*.

Minjoon Seo, Sewon Min, Ali Farhadi, and Hannaneh Hajishirzi. 2017. Query-Reduction Networks for Question Answering. In *Proceedings of the International Conference on Learning Representations (ICLR)*.

Niket Tandon, Bhavana Dalvi, Joel Grus, Wen-tau Yih, Antoine Bosselut, and Peter Clark. 2018. Reasoning about Actions and State Changes by Injecting Commonsense Knowledge. In *Proceedings of the Conference on Empirical Methods in Natural Language Processing (EMNLP)*.

Johannes Welbl, Pontus Stenetorp, and Sebastian Riedel. 2018. Constructing Datasets for Multi-hop Reading Comprehension Across Documents. In *Proceedings of the Transactions of the Association for Computational Linguistics (TACL)*.

Jason Weston, Antoine Bordes, Sumit Chopra, Alexander M Rush, Bart van Merriënboer, Armand Joulin, and Tomas Mikolov. 2015. Towards AI-Complete Question Answering: A Set of Prerequisite Toy Tasks. In *arXiv preprint arXiv:1502.05698*.

Zhilin Yang, Peng Qi, Saizheng Zhang, Yoshua Bengio, William W. Cohen, Ruslan Salakhutdinov, and Christopher D. Manning. 2018. HotpotQA: A Dataset for Diverse, Explainable Multi-hop Question Answering. In *Proceedings of the Conference on Empirical Methods in Natural Language Processing (EMNLP)*.

SPARSE:
Structured Prediction Using Argument-Relative Structured Encoding

Rishi Bommasani
Dept. of Computer Science
Cornell University
rb724@cornell.edu

Arzoo Katiyar
Dept. of Computer Science
Cornell University
arzoo@cs.cornell.edu

Claire Cardie
Dept. of Computer Science
Cornell University
cardie@cs.cornell.edu

Abstract

We propose *structured encoding* as a novel approach to learning representations for relations and events in neural structured prediction. Our approach explicitly leverages the structure of available relation and event metadata to generate these representations, which are parameterized by both the attribute structure of the metadata as well as the learned representation of the arguments of the relations and events. We consider affine, biaffine, and recurrent operators for building hierarchical representations and modelling underlying features.

Without task-specific knowledge sources or domain engineering, we significantly improve over systems and baselines that neglect the available metadata or its hierarchical structure. We observe across-the-board improvements on the BeSt 2016/2017 sentiment analysis task of at least **2.3** (absolute) and **10.6%** (relative) F-measure over the previous state-of-the-art.

1 Introduction

Information extraction has long been an active subarea of natural language processing (NLP) (Onyshkevych et al., 1993; Freitag, 2000). A particularly important class of extraction tasks is ERE detection in which an object, typically an element in a knowledge base, is created for each ENTITY, RELATION, and EVENT identified in a given text (Song et al., 2015). In some variants of ERE detection, *metadata* descriptions and specific *mentions* of the ERE objects also need to be recorded as shown graphically in Figure 1. Subsequent second-order extraction tasks can further build upon first-order ERE information.

In this work, in particular, we consider the second-order structured prediction task studied in the 2016/2017 Belief and Sentiment analysis evaluations (BeSt) (Rambow et al., 2016a): given a document and its EREs (including metadata and mentions) determine the *sentiment* of each ENTITY towards every RELATION and EVENT in the document.[1]

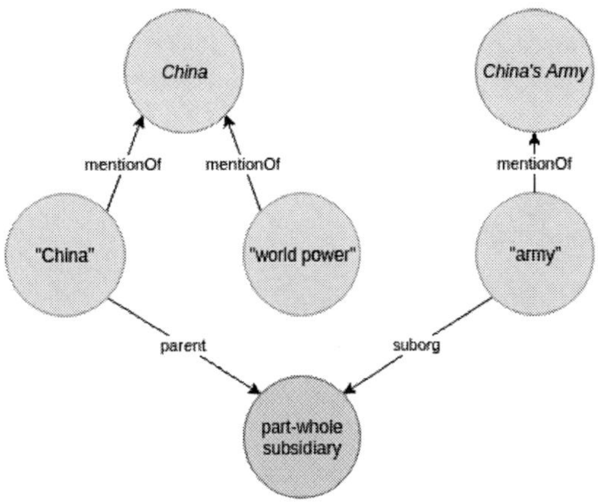

Figure 1: ERE graph for "China, a growing world power, is developing its army." Entities are denoted in blue, entity mentions in green, and relations in red.

Until quite recently, existing approaches to this type of second-order extraction task have relied heavily on domain knowledge and feature engineering (Rambow et al., 2016b; Niculae et al., 2016; Dalton et al., 2016; Gutirrez et al., 2016). And while end-to-end neural network methods that bypass feature engineering have been developed for information extraction problems, they have largely been applied to first-order extraction tasks (Katiyar and Cardie, 2016; Miwa and Bansal, 2016; Katiyar and Cardie, 2017; Orr et al., 2018). Possibly more importantly, these techniques ignore, or have no access to, the internal structure of relations and events.

We hypothesize that utilizing the metadata-

[1]The BeSt evaluation also requires the identification of sentiment towards entities. For reasons that will become clear later, we do not consider entity-to-entity sentiment here.

Proceedings of 3rd Workshop on Structured Prediction for NLP, pages 13–17
Minneapolis, Minnesota, June 7, 2019.

induced structure of relations and events will improve performance on the second-order sentiment analysis task. To this end, we propose *structured encoding* as an approach towards learning representations for relations and events in end-to-end neural structured prediction. In particular, our approach not only models available metadata but also its hierarchical nature.

We evaluate the structured encoding approach on the BeSt 2016/2017 dataset. Without sentiment-specific resources, we are able to see significant improvements over baselines that do not take into account the available structure. We achieve state-of-the-art F1 scores of **22.9** for discussion forum documents and **14.0** for newswire documents. We also openly release our implementation to promote further experimentation and reproducible research.

2 Task Formulation

In the BeSt sentiment analysis setting, we are given a corpus $\mathcal{D}$ where every document $d_i \in \mathcal{D}$ is annotated with the set of entities $\mathcal{E}_i$, relation mentions $\mathcal{R}_i$, and event mentions[2] $\mathcal{EV}_i$ present in d_i. For each entity $e_j \in \mathcal{E}_i$, we are additionally given the *span*, or variable-length n-gram, associated with (each of) its mention(s). Similarly, for each relation and event, we are given metadata specifications of its type and subtype as well as the arguments that constitute it. Our task is then the following: for each potential source-target pair, $(src, trg) \in (\mathcal{E}_i \times \mathcal{R}_i) \cup (\mathcal{E}_i \times \mathcal{EV}_i)$, predict the sentiment (one of POSITIVE, NEGATIVE or NONE) of the src entity towards the trg relation/event.

3 Model

Our structured encoding model is depicted in Figure 2. Its goal is to compute representations for the $\mathbf{src}$, $\mathbf{trg}$, and context $\mathbf{c}$; we then pass the concatenated triple into a FFNN for sentiment classification. We describe the model components in the paragraphs below.

Word and Entity Mention Representation Given a span $s = w_1, \ldots, w_{|s|}$ of the input document, a noncontextual embedding mapping f, and a contextual mapping g, we create the initial word representation $\mathbf{w}_t$ for each word w_t in s by concatenating its noncontextual and contextual

[2]In this work, the distinction between relations/events and relation/event mentions is not considered, so we use 'relation' and 'event' as a shorthand.

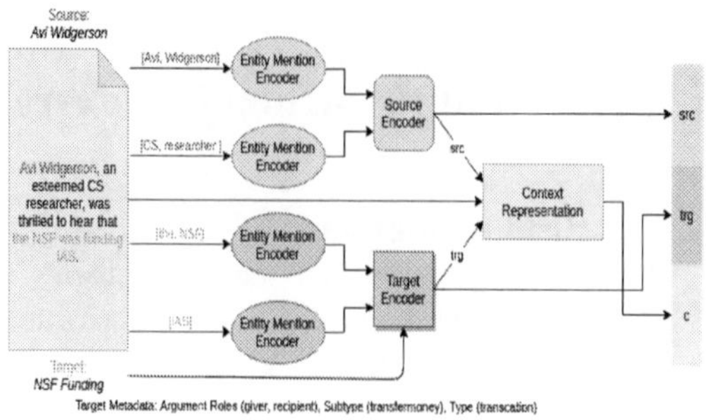

Figure 2: Model for representing the source (blue), target (red), and context (yellow) for the directed sentiment analysis task.

embedding. We then pass the initial word representations through a bidirectional RNN to obtain a domain-specific contextual word representation $\mathbf{h}_t$.[3]

$$\begin{aligned} \mathbf{w}_t &= [f(w_t); g(w_t|s)] \\ \mathbf{h}_t &= [\overrightarrow{RNN}(\mathbf{w}_t); \overleftarrow{RNN}(\mathbf{w}_t)] \end{aligned} \tag{1}$$

For each entity mention s, we compute a representation of s as the mean-pooling of $\mathbf{h}_1, \ldots, \mathbf{h}_{|s|}$.

Source Encoding For each source entity e_j we are given its grounded entity mentions $e_j^1, \ldots, e_j^n$. Similar to the representation methodology for entity-mentions, we represent each source as the average of its entity mention representations.

$$\mathbf{e_j} = \frac{1}{n} \sum_{i=1}^{n} \frac{1}{||[e_j^i]||} \sum_{t=1}^{||[e_j^i]||} \mathbf{h}_t \tag{2}$$

The dataset is also annotated with entities corresponding to the authors of articles. To more appropriately handle these entities, we learn two author embeddings. The *post author* embedding represents the source entity if the target occurs in a post written by the source. If this is not the case, we use the *other author* embedding.

Target Encoding To encode targets, we leverage the hierarchical structure provided in the relation and event metadata. Initially, we construct a fixed-length representation for each of the target's *arguments*, which are *(role, entity mention)* pairs, (r, e_j^k), via concatenation (*flat*) or an affine map (*affine*) as follows (where U_r and $\mathbf{v}_r$ are learned):

$$\begin{aligned} \mathbf{arg}_{j,k}^{r} &= U_r \mathbf{e}_j^k \quad \textit{(affine)} \\ \mathbf{arg}_{j,k}^{r} &= [\mathbf{v}_r; \mathbf{e}_j^k] \quad \textit{(flat)} \end{aligned} \tag{3}$$

For relations, given that the dataset enforces the constraint of two arguments per relation, we pool

[3]This process is not shown in Figure 2.

the relation vectors by concatenating them. On the other hand, for events, as the number of arguments is variable, we propose to pool them with a GRU encoder (Cho et al., 2014). This allows for us to deal with the variable number of arguments and learn compositional relationships between different arguments (arguments are ordered by their semantic roles in the overarching event).

Both relations and events are annotated with their types and subtypes. Based on our hypothesis that hierarchical modeling of structure is important in encoding targets, we consider encoding the subtype and type using *flat* concatenation or learned *affine* maps applied successively in a similar fashion to role encoding for arguments.

Context Representation We encode the source and target independently, capturing the inductive bias that these two components of the input have stand-alone meanings. We find that this is computationally efficient as opposed to approaches that model the source and target on a pair-specific basis. We introduce source-target interaction into the architecture by modeling the textual context in which they appear: first select a source-target specific *context* span; then construct a fixed-length encoding of the *context* using an attention mechanism conditional on the source-target pair. To identify the context span, we identify the closest mention of the source that precedes the target. We begin the context span starting at the first word beyond the end of this mention (w_i). Similarly, we conclude the span at the last word preceding the target (w_j). Denoting the context span as $[w_i, w_j]$, we compute the context vector $\mathbf{c}$ as (where the U maps are learned):

$$\begin{aligned} &\mathbf{u}_{src} = U_{src}\,\mathbf{src};\ \mathbf{u}_{trg} = U_{trg}\,\mathbf{trg};\ \mathbf{u}_t = U_c\,\mathbf{h}_t \\ &\alpha_t = \mathbf{u}_t^T(\mathbf{u}_{src} \odot \mathbf{u}_{trg}) \\ &\alpha = \mathit{softmax}([\alpha_i, \ldots, \alpha_j]^T) \\ &\mathbf{c} = [\mathbf{h}_i, \ldots, \mathbf{h}_j]\alpha \end{aligned} \tag{4}$$

We truncate long spans (length greater than 20) to be the 20 words preceding the start of the target ($i = j - 20$).

4 Results and Analysis

Dataset and Evaluation We use the LDCE114 dataset that was used in the BeSt 2016/2017 English competition. The dataset contains 165 documents, 84 of which are multi-post discussion forums (DF) and 81 are single-post newswire articles (NW), and is summarized in Table 1. We observe that the data is extremely sparse with respect to positive examples: only **0.203%** of all source-target pairs are positive examples with 431 positive examples in 211310 candidate pairs in the training set.

	DF	NW
Length (in num. tokens)	750.36	538.96
Relation Pairs	775.34	1474.51
Relation Positive Examples	1.32	1.02
Event Pairs	810.36	1334.53
Event Positive Examples	2.60	3.98

Table 1: Average document statistics

Consistent with the BeSt evaluation framework, we report the microaverage *adjusted* F1 score[4] and treat NONE as the negative class and both POSITIVE and NEGATIVE as the positive classes. The BeSt metric introduces a notion of partial credit to reward predictions that are incorrect but share global properties with the correct predictions. We find that this metric is well-suited for structured prediction treatments of the task that also consider global structure.

Implementation Details We use frozen word representations that concatenate noncontextual 300-dimensional GloVe embeddings (Pennington et al., 2014) and contextual 3072-dimensional ELMo embeddings (Peters et al., 2018). We use a 2-layer bidirectional LSTM encoder (Hochreiter and Schmidhuber, 1997) and consistently use both a hidden dimensionality of 128 and *tanh* nonlinearities throughout the work. Based on results on the development set, we use an attention dimensionality of 32, a dropout (Srivastava et al., 2014) probability in all hidden layers of 0.2, and a batch size of 10 documents. We also find that a single-layer GRU worked best for event argument pooling and interestingly find that a unidirectional GRU is preferable to a bidirectional GRU. The final classifier is a single-layer FFNN. The model is trained with respect to the class-weighted cross entropy loss where weights are the ℓ_1-normalized vector corresponding to inverse class frequences and optimized using ADAM (Kingma and Ba, 2014) with the default parameters in PyTorch (Paszke et al., 2017). All models are trained for 50 epochs.

[4]Complete results can be found in Appendix A.

			DF	NW
Baseline			14.53	7.24
Columbia/GWU			20.69	10.10
Cornell-Pitt-Michigan			19.48	0.70
Target	Arg	(Sub)Type		
Relation	Flat	Flat	15.2	8.5
Event	Flat	Flat	15.5	8.5
Both	Affine	Affine	**22.9**	**14.0**

Table 2: Experimental results on the BeSt dataset. The specified target types are encoded using *structured encoding* with the specified argument and subtype/type encoding methods. The other target type is encoded with affine maps for the arguments, subtypes, and types.

Overall Results In Table 2, the upper half of the table describes the official BeSt baseline system as well as the top systems on the task. The baseline employs a rule-based heuristic that considers pairs for which the source is the article author as potential positive examples and classifies positive examples as NEGATIVE (the more frequent positive class) (Rambow et al., 2016a). The Columbia/GWU system treats second-order sentiment classification as first-order relation extraction and extends a relation extraction system that uses phrase structure trees, dependency trees, and semantic parses with an SVM using tree kernels (Rambow et al., 2016b). The Cornell-Pitt-Michigan system employs a rule-based heuristic to prune candidate pairs in the sense of link prediction and then performs sentiment classification via multinomial logistic regression (Niculae et al., 2016). They find that the link prediction system sometimes predicts spurious links and permit the classifier to overrule the link prediction judgment by predicting NONE.

Note these results include entities as targets and we argue that this makes the task comparatively easier. In particular, sparsity and dataset size are less of a concern for entity targets as positive examples are equally frequent (**0.196%**) and there are significantly more entity pairs (438165 pairs) than relation and event targets combined (211310 pairs).[5]

In the lower half of Table 2, we report results for different *structured encoding* approaches. As we simultaneously predict sentiment towards relation targets and event targets, we find that the encoding method for one target category tends to improve performance on the other due to shared representations (refer to Appendix A). We find that using affine encoders, which is consistent with the inductive bias of hierarchical encoding, performs best in all settings.

[5]Additionally, entities are unstructured targets and therefore are not well-suited for the contributions of this work.

Embeddings	Encoder	DF	NW
GloVe + ELMo	Bidi-LSTM	**22.9**	**14.0**
GloVe + ELMo*	Bidi-LSTM	8.5	2.4
GloVe	Bidi-LSTM	12.6	8.3
ELMo	Bidi-LSTM	15.0	9.9
GloVe + ELMo	Uni-LSTM	20.9	13.6
GloVe + ELMo	none	22.1	13.6

Table 3: Experimental results on the effects of word representations. * indicates embeddings are not frozen.

Word Representations To understand the effect of pretraining given its pervasive success throughout NLP as well as the extent to which domain-specific LSTM encoders are beneficial, we perform experiments on the development set. When the LSTM encoder is omitted, we introduce an affine projection that yields output vectors of the same dimension as the original LSTM (128). This ensures that the capacity of subsequent model components is unchanged but means there is no domain-specific context modelling. As shown in Table 3, the combination of contextual and noncontextual embeddings leads to an improvement but the contextual embeddings perform better stand-alone. In doing this comparison, we consider pretrained embeddings of differing dimensionalities however since in most settings the embeddings are frozen, we do not find that this significantly effects the run time or model capacity. When embeddings are learned, we observe a substantial decline in performance which we posit is due to catastrophic forgetting due to noisy and erratic signal from the loss. The results further indicate that a bidirectional task oriented encoder improves performance.

5 Conclusion

In this paper, we propose *structured encoding* to model structured targets in semantic link prediction. We demonstrate that this framework along with pretrained word embeddings can be an effective combination as we achieve state-of-the-art performance on several metrics in the BeSt 2016/2017 Task in English.

Acknowledgements

We thank Vlad Niculae for his tremendous support and guidance in the early stages of this work and RB especially thanks him for his advice on research and for being the gold standard for code quality. We thank the anonymous reviewers for their insightful feedback.

References

Kyunghyun Cho, Bart van Merrienboer, Çaglar Gülçehre, Fethi Bougares, Holger Schwenk, and Yoshua Bengio. 2014. Learning phrase representations using RNN encoder-decoder for statistical machine translation. *CoRR*, abs/1406.1078.

Adam Dalton, Morgan Wixted, Yorick Wilks, Meenakshi Alagesan, Gregorios Katsios, Ananya Subburathinam, and Tomek Strzalkowski. 2016. Target-focused sentiment and belief extraction and classification using cubism. In *TAC*.

Dayne Freitag. 2000. Machine learning for information extraction in informal domains. *Machine Learning*, 39(2):169–202.

Yoan Gutirrez, Salud Mara Jimnez-Zafra, Isabel Moreno, M. Teresa Martn-Valdivia, David Toms, Arturo Montejo-Rez, Andrs Montoyo, L. Alfonso Urea-Lpez, Patricio Martnez-Barco, Fernando Martnez-Santiago, Rafael Muoz, and Eladio Blanco-Lpez. 2016. Redes at tac knowledge base population 2016: Edl and best tracks. In *TAC*.

Sepp Hochreiter and Jürgen Schmidhuber. 1997. Long short-term memory. *Neural Comput.*, 9(8):1735–1780.

Arzoo Katiyar and Claire Cardie. 2016. Investigating lstms for joint extraction of opinion entities and relations. In *Proceedings of the 54th Annual Meeting of the Association for Computational Linguistics (Volume 1: Long Papers)*, pages 919–929. Association for Computational Linguistics.

Arzoo Katiyar and Claire Cardie. 2017. Going out on a limb: Joint extraction of entity mentions and relations without dependency trees. In *Proceedings of the 55th Annual Meeting of the Association for Computational Linguistics (Volume 1: Long Papers)*, pages 917–928. Association for Computational Linguistics.

Diederik P. Kingma and Jimmy Ba. 2014. Adam: A method for stochastic optimization. *CoRR*, abs/1412.6980.

Makoto Miwa and Mohit Bansal. 2016. End-to-end relation extraction using lstms on sequences and tree structures. In *Proceedings of the 54th Annual Meeting of the Association for Computational Linguistics (Volume 1: Long Papers)*, pages 1105–1116. Association for Computational Linguistics.

Vlad Niculae, Kai Sun, Xilun Chen, Yao Cheng, Xinya Du, Esin Durmus, Arzoo Katiyar, and Claire Cardie. 2016. Cornell belief and sentiment system at tac 2016. In *TAC*.

Boyan Onyshkevych, Mary Ellen Okurowski, and Lynn Carlson. 1993. Tasks, domains, and languages for information extraction. In *Proceedings of a workshop on held at Fredericksburg, Virginia: September 19-23, 1993*, pages 123–133. Association for Computational Linguistics.

Walker Orr, Prasad Tadepalli, and Xiaoli Fern. 2018. Event detection with neural networks: A rigorous empirical evaluation. In *Proceedings of the 2018 Conference on Empirical Methods in Natural Language Processing*, pages 999–1004. Association for Computational Linguistics.

Adam Paszke, Sam Gross, Soumith Chintala, Gregory Chanan, Edward Yang, Zachary DeVito, Zeming Lin, Alban Desmaison, Luca Antiga, and Adam Lerer. 2017. Automatic differentiation in pytorch.

Jeffrey Pennington, Richard Socher, and Christopher D. Manning. 2014. Glove: Global vectors for word representation. In *Empirical Methods in Natural Language Processing (EMNLP)*, pages 1532–1543.

Matthew E. Peters, Mark Neumann, Mohit Iyyer, Matt Gardner, Christopher Clark, Kenton Lee, and Luke Zettlemoyer. 2018. Deep contextualized word representations. In *Proc. of NAACL*.

Owen Rambow, Meenakshi Alagesan, Michael Arrigo, Daniel Bauer, Claire Cardie, Adam Dalton, Mona Diab, Greg Dubbin, Gregorios Katsios, Axinia Radeva, Tomek Strzalkowski, and Jennifer Tracey. 2016a. The 2016 tac kbp best evaluation. In *TAC*.

Owen Rambow, Tao Yu, Axinia Radeva, Alexander Richard Fabbri, Christopher Hidey, Tianrui Peng, Kathleen McKeown, Smaranda Muresan, Sardar Hamidian, Mona T. Diab, and Debanjan Ghosh. 2016b. The columbia-gwu system at the 2016 tac kbp best evaluation. In *TAC*.

Zhiyi Song, Ann Bies, Stephanie Strassel, Tom Riese, Justin Mott, Joe Ellis, Jonathan Wright, Seth Kulick, Neville Ryant, and Xiaoyi Ma. 2015. From light to rich ere: annotation of entities, relations, and events. In *Proceedings of the the 3rd Workshop on EVENTS: Definition, Detection, Coreference, and Representation*, pages 89–98.

Nitish Srivastava, Geoffrey Hinton, Alex Krizhevsky, Ilya Sutskever, and Ruslan Salakhutdinov. 2014. Dropout: A simple way to prevent neural networks from overfitting. *J. Mach. Learn. Res.*, 15(1):1929–1958.

Lightly-supervised Representation Learning with Global Interpretability

Andrew Zupon, Maria Alexeeva, Marco A. Valenzuela-Escárcega,
Ajay Nagesh, and **Mihai Surdeanu**
University of Arizona, Tucson, AZ, USA
{zupon, alexeeva, marcov, ajaynagesh, msurdeanu}
@email.arizona.edu

Abstract

We propose a lightly-supervised approach for information extraction, in particular named entity classification, which combines the benefits of traditional bootstrapping, i.e., use of limited annotations and interpretability of extraction patterns, with the robust learning approaches proposed in representation learning. Our algorithm iteratively learns custom embeddings for both the multi-word entities to be extracted and the patterns that match them from a few example entities per category. We demonstrate that this representation-based approach outperforms three other state-of-the-art bootstrapping approaches on two datasets: CoNLL-2003 and OntoNotes. Additionally, using these embeddings, our approach outputs a globally-interpretable model consisting of a decision list, by ranking patterns based on their proximity to the average entity embedding in a given class. We show that this interpretable model performs close to our complete bootstrapping model, proving that representation learning can be used to produce interpretable models with small loss in performance. This decision list can be edited by human experts to mitigate some of that loss and in some cases outperform the original model.

1 Introduction

One strategy for mitigating the cost of supervised learning in information extraction (IE) is to bootstrap extractors with light supervision from a few provided examples (or seeds). Traditionally, bootstrapping approaches iterate between learning extraction patterns such as word n-grams, e.g., the pattern "`@ENTITY , former president`" could be used to extract person names,[1] and applying these patterns to extract the desired structures (entities, relations, etc.) (Carlson et al., 2010; Gupta and Manning, 2014, 2015, inter alia). One advantage of this direction is that these patterns are interpretable, which mitigates the maintenance cost associated with machine learning systems (Sculley et al., 2014).

On the other hand, representation learning has proven to be useful for natural language processing (NLP) applications (Mikolov et al., 2013; Riedel et al., 2013; Toutanova et al., 2015, 2016, inter alia). Representation learning approaches often include a component that is trained in an unsupervised manner, e.g., predicting words based on their context from large amounts of data, mitigating the brittle statistics affecting traditional bootstrapping approaches. However, the resulting real-valued embedding vectors are hard to interpret.

Here we argue that these two directions are complementary, and should be combined. We propose such a bootstrapping approach for information extraction (IE), which blends the advantages of both directions. As a use case, we instantiate our idea for named entity classification (NEC), i.e., classifying a given set of unknown entities into a predefined set of categories (Collins and Singer, 1999). The contributions of this work are:

(1) We propose an approach for bootstrapping NEC that iteratively learns custom embeddings for *both* the multi-word entities to be extracted and the patterns that match them from a few example entities per category. Our approach changes the objective function of a neural network language models (NNLM) to include a semi-supervised component that models the known examples, i.e., by *attracting* entities and patterns in the same category to each other and *repelling* them from elements in different categories, and it adds an external iterative process that "cautiously" augments the pools of known examples (Collins and Singer, 1999). In other words, our contribution is an example of combining representation learning and bootstrapping.

(2) We demonstrate that our representation learn-

[1] In this work we use surface patterns, but the proposed algorithm is agnostic to the types of patterns learned.

Proceedings of 3rd Workshop on Structured Prediction for NLP, pages 18–28
Minneapolis, Minnesota, June 7, 2019.

ing approach is suitable for semi-supervised NEC. We compare our approach against several state-of-the-art semi-supervised approaches on two datasets: CoNLL-2003 (Tjong Kim Sang and De Meulder, 2003) and OntoNotes (Pradhan et al., 2013). We show that, despite its simplicity, our method outperforms all other approaches.

(3) Our approach also outputs an interpretation of the learned model, consisting of a decision list of patterns, where each pattern gets a score per class based on the proximity of its embedding to the average entity embedding in the given class. This interpretation is global, i.e., it explains the entire model rather than local predictions. We show that this decision-list model performs comparably to the complete model on the two datasets.

(4) We also demonstrate that the resulting system can be understood, debugged, and maintained by non-machine learning experts. We compare the decision-list model edited by human domain experts with the unedited decision-list model and see a modest improvement in overall performance, with some categories getting a bigger boost. This improvement shows that, for non-ambiguous categories that are well-defined by the local contexts captured by our patterns, these patterns truly are interpretable to end users.

2 Related Work

Bootstrapping is an iterative process that alternates between learning representative patterns, and acquiring new entities (or relations) belonging to a given category (Riloff, 1996; McIntosh, 2010). Patterns and extractions are ranked using either formulas that measure their frequency and association with a category, or classifiers, which increases robustness due to regularization (Carlson et al., 2010; Gupta and Manning, 2015). While semi-supervised learning is not novel (Yarowsky, 1995; Gupta and Manning, 2014), our approach performs better than some modern implementations of these methids such as Gupta and Manning (2014).

Distributed representations of words (Deerwester et al., 1990; Mikolov et al., 2013; Levy and Goldberg, 2014) serve as underlying representation for many NLP tasks such as information extraction and question answering (Riedel et al., 2013; Toutanova et al., 2015, 2016; Sharp et al., 2016). Mrkšić et al. (2017) build on traditional distributional models by incorporating synonymy and antonymy relations as supervision to fine tune word vector spaces, using an Attract/Repel method similar to our idea. However, most of these works that customize embeddings for a specific task rely on some form of supervision. In contrast, our approach is lightly supervised, with a only few seed examples per category. Batista et al. (2015) perform bootstrapping for relation extraction using pre-trained word embeddings. They do not learn custom pattern embeddings that apply to multi-word entities and patterns. We show that customizing embeddings for the learned patterns is important for interpretability.

Recent work has focused on explanations of machine learning models that are model-agnostic but local, i.e., they interpret individual model predictions (Ribeiro et al., 2018, 2016a). In contrast, our work produces a global interpretation, which explains the entire extraction model rather than individual decisions.

Lastly, our work addresses the interpretability aspect of information extraction methods. Interpretable models mitigate the technical debt of machine learning (Sculley et al., 2014). For example, it allows domain experts to make manual, gradual improvements to the models. This is why rule-based approaches are commonly used in industry applications, where software maintenance is crucial (Chiticariu et al., 2013). Furthermore, the need for interpretability also arises in critical systems, e.g., recommending treatment to patients, where these systems are deployed to aid human decision makers (Lakkaraju and Rudin, 2016). The benefits of interpretability have encouraged efforts to either extract interpretable models from opaque ones (Craven and Shavlik, 1996), or to explain their decisions (Ribeiro et al., 2016b).

As machine learning models are becoming more complex, the focus on interpretability has become more important, with new funding programs focused on this topic.[2] Our approach for exporting an interpretable model (§3) is similar to Valenzuela-Escárcega et al. (2016), but we start from distributed representations, whereas they started from a logistic regression model with explicit features.

[2] DARPA's Explainable AI program: `http://www.darpa.mil/program/explainable-artificial-intelligence`.

3 Approach

Bootstrapping with representation learning

Our algorithm iteratively grows a pool of multi-word entities (entPool_c) and n-gram patterns (patPool_c) for each category of interest c, and learns custom embeddings for both, which we will show are crucial for both performance and interpretability.

The entity pools are initialized with a few seed examples (seeds_c) for each category. For example, in our experiments we initialize the pool for a `person names` category with 10 names such as *Mother Teresa*. Then the algorithm iteratively applies the following three steps for T epochs:

(1) *Learning custom embeddings*: The algorithm learns custom embeddings for all entities and patterns in the dataset, using the current entPool_cs as supervision. This is a key contribution, and is detailed in the second part of this section.

(2) *Pattern promotion*: We generate the patterns that match the entities in each pool entPool_c, rank those patterns using point-wise mutual information (PMI) with the corresponding category, and select the top ranked patterns for promotion to the corresponding pattern pool patPool_c. In this work, we use use surface patterns consisting of up to 4 words before/after the entity of interest, e.g., the pattern "`@ENTITY , former president`" matches any entity followed by the three tokens ,, *former*, and *president*. However, our method is agnostic to the types of patterns learned, and can be trivially adapted to other types of patterns, e.g., over sytactic dependency paths.

(3) *Entity promotion*: Entities are promoted to entPool_c using a multi-class classifier that estimates the likelihood of an entity belonging to each class (Gupta and Manning, 2015). Our feature set includes, for each category c: (a) edit distance over characters between the candidate entity e and current $e_c\text{s} \in \text{entPool}_c$, (b) the PMI (with c) of the patterns in patPool_c that matched e in the training documents, and (c) similarity between e and e_cs in a semantic space. For the latter feature group, we use the set of embedding vectors learned in step (1). These features are taken from Gupta and Manning (2015). We use these vectors to compute the cosine similarity score of a given candidate entity e to the entities in entPool_c, and add the average and maximum similarities as features. The top 10 entities classified with the highest confidence for each class are promoted to the corresponding entPool_c after each epoch.

Learning custom embeddings

We train our embeddings for both entities and patterns by maximizing the objective function J:

$$J = \text{SG} + \text{Attract} + \text{Repel} \quad (1)$$

where SG, Attract, and Repel are individual components of the objective function designed to model both the unsupervised, language model part of the task as well as the light supervision coming from the seed examples, as detailed below. A similar approach is proposed by (Mrkšić et al., 2017), who use an objective function modified with Attract and Repel components to fine-tune word embeddings with synonym and antonym pairs.

The SG term is formulated identically to the original objective function of the *S*kip-*G*ram model of Mikolov et al. (2013), but, crucially, adapted to operate over multi-word entities and contexts consisting not of bags of context words, but of the patterns that match each entity. Thus, intuitively, our SG term encourages the embeddings of entities to be similar to the embeddings of the patterns matching them:

$$\begin{aligned} \text{SG} = \sum_e [&\log(\sigma(V_e^\top V_{pp})) + \\ &\sum_{np} \log(\sigma(-V_e^\top V_{np}))] \end{aligned} \quad (2)$$

where e represents an entity, pp represents a positive pattern, i.e., a pattern that matches entity e in the training texts, np represents a negative pattern, i.e., it has not been seen with this entity, and σ is the sigmoid function. Intuitively, this component forces the embeddings of entities to be similar to the embeddings of the patterns that match them, and dissimilar to the negative patterns.

The second component, Attract, encourages entities or patterns in the same pool to be close to each other. For example, if we have two entities in the pool known to be person names, they should be close to each other in the embedding space:

$$\text{Attract} = \sum_P \sum_{x1,x2 \in P} \log(\sigma(V_{x1}^\top V_{x2})) \quad (3)$$

where P is the entity/pattern pool for a category, and $x1, x2$ are entities/patterns in said pool.

Lastly, the third term, Repel, encourages that the pools be mutually exclusive, which is a soft version of the counter training approach of Yangarber (2003) or the weighted mutual-exclusive bootstrapping algorithm of McIntosh and Curran (2008). For example, person names should be far from organization names in the semantic embedding space:

$$\text{Repel} = \sum_{P1,P2 \text{ if } P1 \neq P2} \sum_{x1 \in P1} \sum_{x2 \in P2} \log(\sigma(-V_{x1}^{\top} V_{x2})) \quad (4)$$

where $P1, P2$ are different pools, and $x1$ and $x2$ are entities/patterns in $P1$, and $P2$, respectively.

We term the complete algorithm that learns and uses custom embeddings as *Emboot* (*Em*beddings for *boot*strapping), and the stripped-down version without them as *EPB* (*E*xplicit *P*attern-based *B*ootstrapping). EPB is similar to Gupta and Manning (2015); the main difference is that we use pretrained embeddings in the entity promotion classifier rather than Brown clusters. In other words, EPB relies on pretrained embeddings for both patterns and entities rather than the custom ones that Emboot learns.[3]

Interpretable model

In addition to its output (entPool$_c$s), Emboot produces custom entity and pattern embeddings that can be used to construct a decision-list model, which provides a global, deterministic interpretation of what Emboot learned.

This interpretable model is constructed as follows. First, we produce an average embedding per category by averaging the embeddings of the entities in each entPool$_c$. Second, we estimate the cosine similarity between each of the pattern embeddings and these category embeddings, and convert them to a probability distribution using a softmax function; $prob_c(p)$ is the resulting probability of pattern p for class c.

After being constructed, the interpretable model is used as follows. First, each candidate entity to be classified, e, receives a score for a given class c from all patterns in patPool$_c$ that match it. The entity score aggregates the relevant pattern probabilities using Noisy-Or:

$$Score(e, c) = 1 - \prod_{\{p_c \in patPool_c | matches(p_c, e)\}} (1 - prob_c(p_c)) \quad (5)$$

Each entity is then assigned to the category with the highest overall score.

4 Experiments

We evaluate the above algorithms on the task of named entity classification from free text.

Datasets: We used two datasets, the CoNLL-2003 shared task dataset (Tjong Kim Sang and De Meulder, 2003), which contains 4 entity types, and the OntoNotes dataset (Pradhan et al., 2013), which contains 11.[4] These datasets contain marked entity boundaries with labels for each marked entity. Here we only use the entity boundaries but *not* the labels of these entities during the training of our bootstrapping systems. To simulate learning from large texts, we tuned hyper parameters on development, but ran the actual experiments on the *train* partitions.

Baselines: In addition to the EPB algorithm, we compare against the approach proposed by Gupta and Manning (2014)[5]. This algorithm is a simpler version of the EPB system, where entities are promoted with a PMI-based formula rather than an entity classifier.[6] Further, we compare against label propagation (LP) (Zhu and Ghahramani, 2002), with the implementation available in the `scikit-learn` package.[7] In each bootstrapping epoch, we run LP, select the entities with the lowest entropy, and add them to their top category. Each entity is represented by a feature vector that contains the co-occurrence counts of the entity and each of the patterns that matches it in text.[8]

Settings: For all baselines and proposed models, we used the same set of 10 seeds/category, which were manually chosen from the most frequent entities in the dataset. For the custom embedding

[3]For multi-word entities and patterns, we simply average word embeddings to generate entity and pattern embeddings for EPB.

[4]We excluded numerical categories such as DATE.

[5]https://nlp.stanford.edu/software/patternslearning.shtml

[6]We did not run this system on OntoNotes dataset as it uses a builtin NE classifier with a predefined set of labels which did not match the OntoNotes labels.

[7]http://scikit-learn.org/stable/modules/generated/sklearn.semi_supervised.LabelPropagation.html

[8]We experimented with other feature values, e.g., pattern PMI scores, but all performed worse than raw counts.

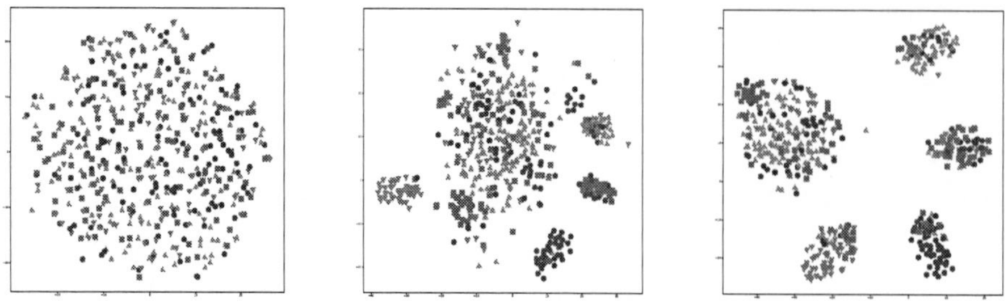

(a) Embeddings initialized randomly (b) Bootstrapping epoch 5 (c) Bootstrapping epoch 10

Figure 1: t-SNE visualizations of the entity embeddings at three stages during training. Legend: ● = LOC. ■ = ORG. ▲ = PER. ▼ = MISC. This figure is best viewed in color.

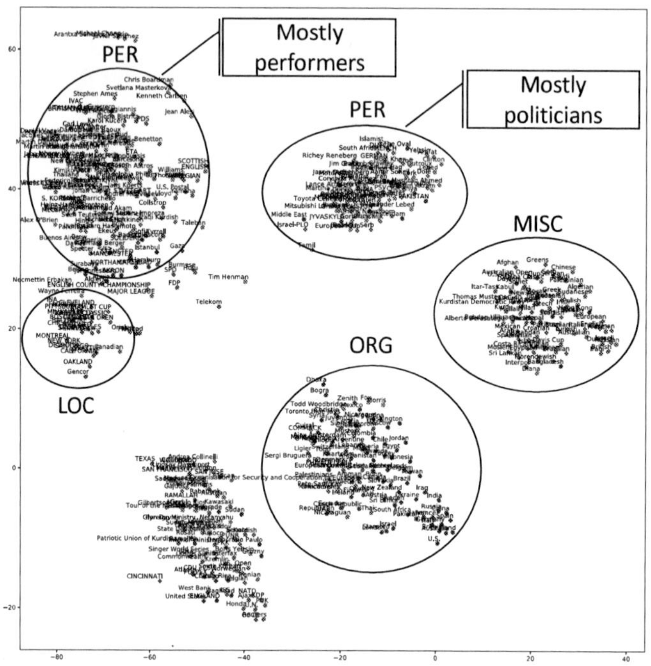

Figure 2: t-SNE visualizations of the entity embeddings learned by Emboot after training completes. Legend: ● = LOC. ● = ORG. ● = PER. ● = MISC.

features, we used randomly initialized 15d embeddings. Here we consider patterns to be n-grams of size up to 4 tokens on either side of an entity. For instance, "`@ENTITY , former President`" is one of the patterns learned for the class `person`. We ran all algorithms for 20 bootstrapping epochs, and the embedding learning component for 100 epochs in each bootstrapping epoch. We add 10 entities and 10 patterns to each category during every bootstrapping epoch.

5 Discussion

Qualitative Analysis

Before we discuss overall results, we provide a qualitative analysis of the learning process for Emboot for the CoNLL dataset in Figure 1. The figure shows t-SNE visualizations (van der Maaten and Hinton, 2008) of the entity embeddings at several stages of the algorithm. This visualization matches our intuition: as training advances, entities belonging to the same category are indeed grouped together. In particular, Figure 1c shows five clusters, four of which are dominated by one category (and centered around the corresponding seeds), and one, in the upper left corner, with the entities that haven't yet been added to any of the pools.

Figure 2 shows a more detailed view of the t-SNE projections of entity embeddings after Emboot's training completes. Again, this demonstrates that Emboot's semi-supervised approach clusters most entities based on their (unseen) categories. Interestingly, Emboot learned two clusters for the PER category. Upon a manual inspection of these clusters, we observed that one contains mostly performers (e.g., athletes or artists such as Stephen Ames, a professional golfer), while the other contains many politicians (e.g., Arafat and Clinton). Thus, Emboot learned correctly that, at least at the time when the CoNLL 2003 dataset was created, the context in which politicians and performers were mentioned was different. The cluster in the bottom left part of the figure contains the remaining working pool of patterns, which were not assigned to any category cluster after the training epochs.

Quantitative Analysis

A quantitative comparison of the different models on the two datasets is shown in Figure 3.

Figure 3 shows that Emboot considerably outperforms LP and Gupta and Manning (2014), and has an occasional improvement over EPB. While EPB sometimes outperforms Emboot, Emboot has the potential for manual curation of its model, which we will explore later in this section. This demonstrates the value of our approach, and the importance of custom embeddings.

Importantly, we compare Emboot against: (a) its interpretable version ($\text{Emboot}_{\text{int}}$), which is constructed as a decision list containing the patterns learned (and scored) after each bootstrapping epoch, and (b) an interpretable system built similarly for EPB (EPB_{int}), using the pretrained Levy and Goldberg embeddings[9] rather than our custom ones. This analysis shows that $\text{Emboot}_{\text{int}}$ performs close to Emboot on both datasets, demonstrating that most of the benefits of representation learning are available in an interpretable model. Please see the discussion on the edited interpretable model in the next section.

Importantly, the figure also shows that EPB_{int}, which uses generic entity embeddings rather than the custom ones learned for the task performs considerably worse than the other approaches. This highlights the importance of learning a dedicated distributed representation for this task.

Interpretability Analysis

Is the list of patterns generated by the interpretable model actually interpretable to end users? To investigate this, we asked two linguists to curate the models learned by $\text{Emboot}_{\text{int}}$, by editing the list of patterns in a given model. First, the experts performed an independent analysis of all the patterns. Next, the two experts conferred with each other and came to a consensus when their independent decisions on a particular pattern disagreed. These first two stages took the experts 2 hours for the CoNLL dataset and 3 hours for the OntoNotes dataset. The experts did not have access to the original texts the patterns were pulled from, so they had to make their decisions based on the patterns alone. They made one of three decisions for each pattern: (1) no change, when the pattern is a good fit for the category; (2) changing the category, when the pattern clearly belongs to a different category; and (3) deleting the pattern, when the pattern is either not informative enough for any category or when the pattern could occur with entities from multiple categories. The experts did not have the option of modifying the content of the pattern, because each pattern is associated with an embedding learned during training. Table 1 shows several examples of the patterns and decision made by the annotators. A summary of the changes made for the CoNLL dataset is given in Figure 4, and a summary of the changes made for the OntoNotes dataset is given in Figure 5.

As Figure 3 shows, this edited interpretable model ($\text{Emboot}_{\text{int-edited}}$) performs similarly to the unedited interpretable model. When we look a little deeper, the observed overall similarity between the unchanged and the edited interpretable Emboot models for both datasets depends on the specific categories and the specific patterns involved. For example, when we look at the CoNLL dataset, we observe that the edited model outperforms the unchanged model on PER entities, but performs worse than the unchanged model on ORG enti-

[9]For multi-word entities, we averaged the embeddings of the individual words in the entity to create an overall entity embedding.

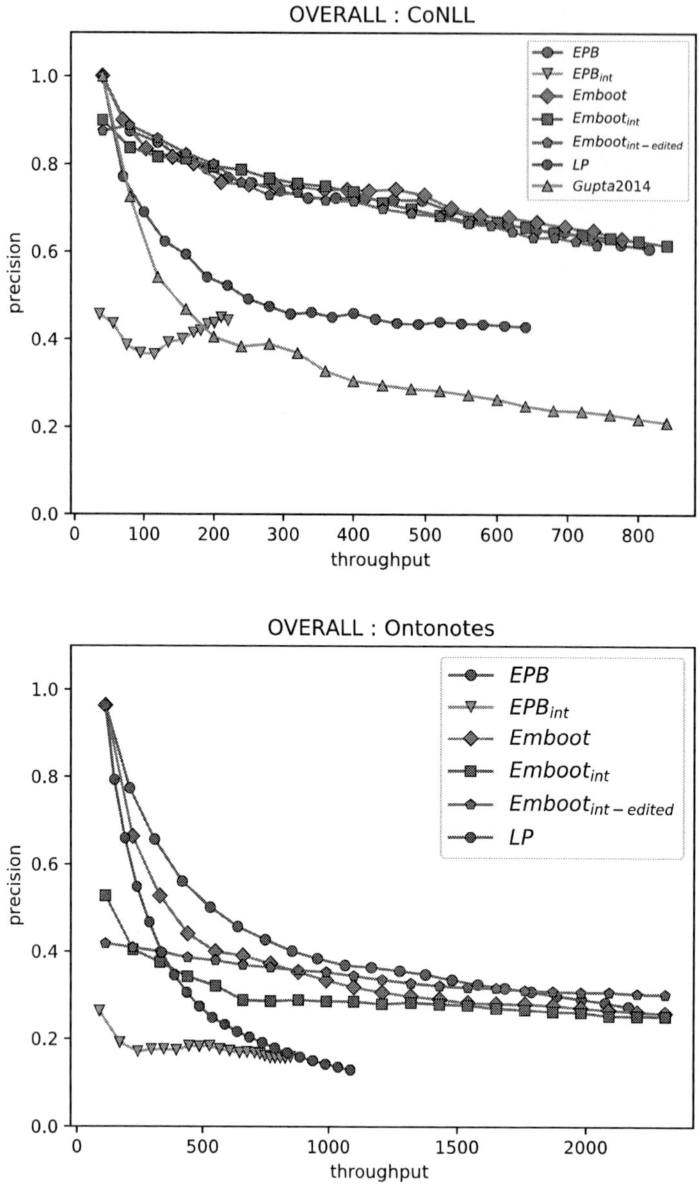

Figure 3: Overall results on the CoNLL and OntoNotes datasets. Throughput is the number of entities classified, and precision is the proportion of entities that were classified correctly. Please see Sec. 4 for a description of the systems listed in the legend.

Pattern	Original Label	Decision	Rationale
@ENTITY was the	LOC	delete	the pattern is too broad
@ENTITY) Ferrari	LOC	delete	the pattern is uninformative
citizen of @ENTITY	MISC	change to LOC	the pattern is more likely to occur with a location
According to @ENTITY officials	ORG	no change	the pattern is likely to occur with an organization

Table 1: Examples of patterns and experts' decisions and rationales from the CoNLL dataset.

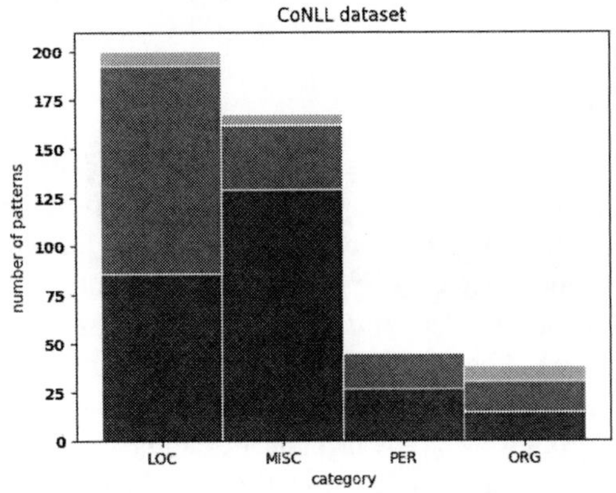

Figure 4: Summary of expert decisions when editing the $\text{Emboot}_{\text{int}}$ model, for the CoNLL dataset by original category. Dark blue (bottom) is no change, medium blue (middle) is deletions, light blue (top) is change of category.

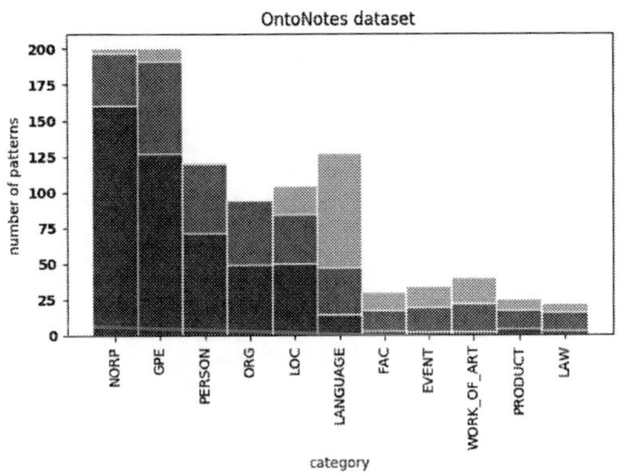

Figure 5: Summary of expert decisions when editing the $\text{Emboot}_{\text{int}}$ model, for the OntoNotes dataset by original category. Dark blue (bottom) is no change, medium blue (middle) is deletions, light blue (top) is change of category.

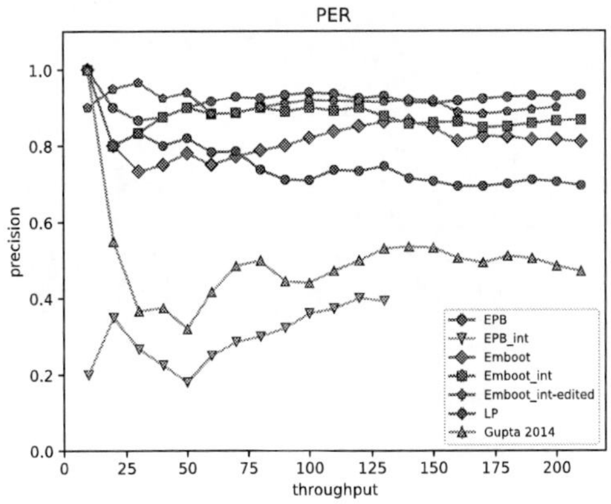

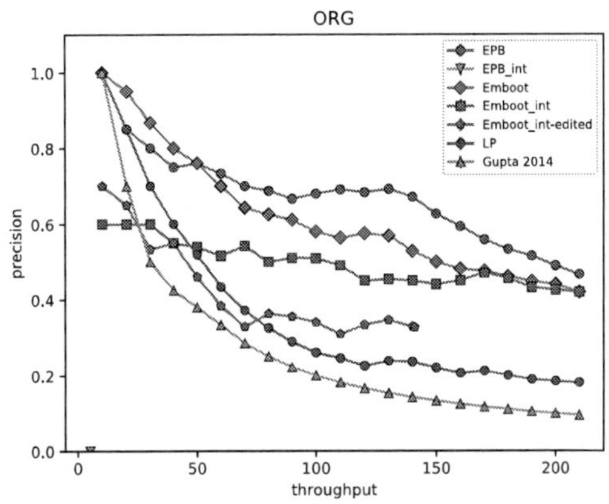

Figure 6: CoNLL results for PER and ORG. The $\text{Emboot}_{\text{int-edited}}$ model generally outperforms the $\text{Emboot}_{\text{int}}$ model when it comes to PER entities, but not for ORG entities. This discrepancy seems to relate to the amount of local information available in PER patterns versus ORG patterns that can aid human domain experts in correcting the patterns. The EPB_{int} model (incorrectly) classifies very few entities as ORG, which is why it only shows up as a single point in the bottom left of the lower plot.

ties (Figure 6). We observe a similar pattern with the OntoNotes dataset, where the $\text{Emboot}_{\text{int-edited}}$ model outperforms the $\text{Emboot}_{\text{int}}$ model greatly for GPE but not for LAW (Figure 7). Overall, for OntoNotes, $\text{Emboot}_{\text{int-edited}}$ outperforms $\text{Emboot}_{\text{int}}$ for 5 categories out of 11. For the categories where $\text{Emboot}_{\text{int-edited}}$ performs worse, the data is sparse, so few patterns are promoted (30 FAC patterns compared to 200 GPE patterns), and many of them were deleted or changed by the two linguists (14 FAC deletions and 13 FAC changes, with only 3 FAC patterns remaining).

This difference in outcome partially has to do with the amount of *local* vs. *global* information available in the patterns. For example, local patterns are common for the PER and MISC categories in CoNLL, and for the GPE category in OntoNotes, e.g., the entity "Syrian" is correctly classified as MISC (which includes demonyms) due to two patterns matching it in the CoNLL dataset: "`@ENTITY President`" and "`@ENTITY troops`". In general, the majority of predictions are triggered by 1 or 2 patterns, which makes these decisions explainable. For the CoNLL dataset, 59% of $\text{Emboot}_{\text{int}}$'s predictions are triggered by 1 or 2 patterns; 84% are generated by 5 or fewer patterns; only 1.1% of predictions are generated by 10 or more patterns.

On the other hand, without seeing the full source text, the experts were not able to

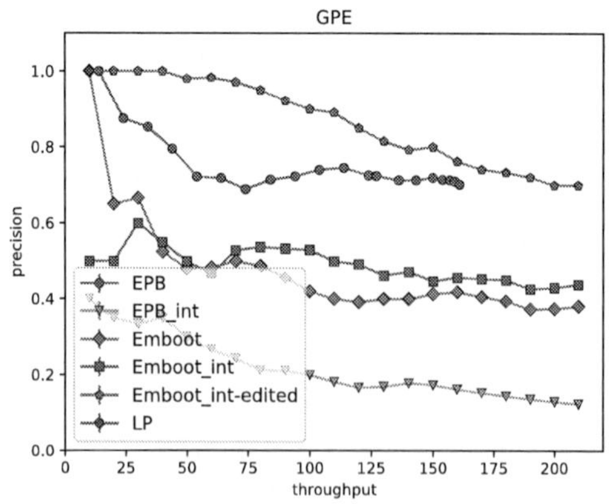

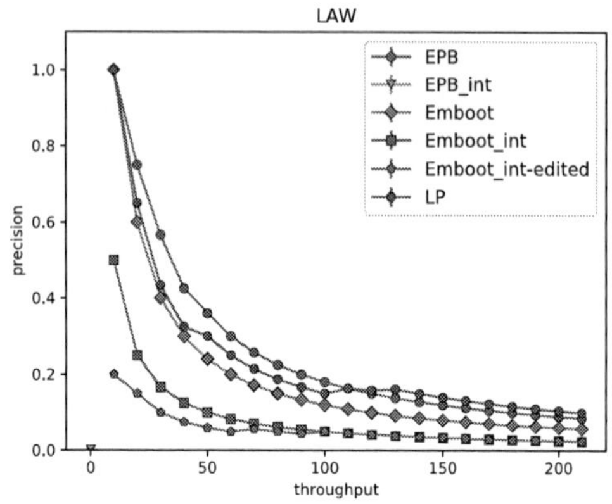

Figure 7: OntoNotes results for GPE and LAW. The $\text{Emboot}_{\text{int-edited}}$ model greatly outperforms both Emboot and $\text{Emboot}_{\text{int}}$ models when it comes to GPE entities, but not for LAW entities. This discrepancy seems to relate to the amount of local information available in GPE patterns versus LAW patterns that can aid human domain experts in correcting the patterns. EPB_{int} does not classify any entities as LAW.

make an accurate judgment on the validity of some patterns—for instance, while the pattern `@ENTITY and Portugal` clearly indicates a geo-political entity, the pattern `@ENTITY has been` (labeled `facility` originally when training on OntoNotes documents) can co-occur with entities from any category. Such patterns are common for the LAW category in OntoNotes, and for the ORG category in CoNLL (due to the focus on sport events in CoNLL, where location names are commonly used as a placeholder for the corresponding team), which partially explains the poor curation results on these categories in Figures 6 and 7. Additionally, lower performance on certain categories can be partially explained by the small amount of data in those categories and the fact that the edits made by the experts drastically changed the number of patterns that occur with some categories (see Figures 4 and 5).

6 Conclusion

This work introduced an example of representation learning being successfully combined with traditional, pattern-based bootstrapping for information extraction, in particular named entity classification. Our approach iteratively learns custom embeddings for multi-word entities and the patterns that match them as well as cautiously augmenting the pools of known examples. This approach outperforms several state-of-the-art semi-supervised approaches to NEC on two datasets, CoNLL 2003 and OntoNotes.

Our approach can also export the model learned into an interpretable list of patterns, which human domain experts can use to understand why an extraction was generated. These patterns can be manually curated to improve the performance of the system by modifying the model directly, with minimal effort. For example, we used a team of two linguists to curate the model learned for OntoNotes in 3 hours. The model edited by human domain experts shows a modest improvement over the unedited model, demonstrating the usefulness of these interpretable patterns. Interestingly, the manual curation of these patterns performed better for some categories that rely mostly on local context that is captured by the type of patterns used in this work, and less well for categories that require global context that is beyond the n-gram patterns used here. This observation raises opportunities for future work such as how to learn global context in an interpretable way, and how to adjust the amount of global information depending on the category learned.

7 Acknowledgments

We gratefully thank Yoav Goldberg for his suggestions for the manual curation experiments.

This work was supported by the Defense Advanced Research Projects Agency (DARPA) under the Big Mechanism program, grant W911NF-14-1-0395, and by the Bill and Melinda Gates Foundation HBGDki Initiative. Marco Valenzuela-Escárcega and Mihai Surdeanu declare a financial interest in lum.ai. This interest has been properly disclosed to the University of Arizona Institutional Review Committee and is managed in accordance with its conflict of interest policies.

References

David S Batista, Bruno Martins, and Mário J Silva. 2015. Semi-supervised bootstrapping of relationship extractors with distributional semantics. In *In Empirical Methods in Natural Language Processing*. ACL.

Andrew Carlson, Justin Betteridge, Richard C Wang, Estevam R Hruschka Jr, and Tom M Mitchell. 2010. Coupled semi-supervised learning for information extraction. In *Proceedings of the third ACM international conference on Web search and data mining*, pages 101–110. ACM.

Laura Chiticariu, Yunyao Li, and Frederick R Reiss. 2013. Rule-based information extraction is dead! long live rule-based information extraction systems! In *EMNLP*, October, pages 827–832.

Michael Collins and Yoram Singer. 1999. Unsupervised models for named entity classification. In *Proceedings of the Conference on Empirical Methods in Natural Language Processing*.

Mark W Craven and Jude W Shavlik. 1996. Extracting tree-structured representations of trained networks. *Advances in neural information processing systems*, pages 24–30.

Scott Deerwester, Susan T Dumais, George W Furnas, Thomas K Landauer, and Richard Harshman. 1990. Indexing by latent semantic analysis. *Journal of the American society for information science*, 41(6):391–407.

Sonal Gupta and Christopher D Manning. 2014. Improved pattern learning for bootstrapped entity extraction. In *CoNLL*, pages 98–108.

Sonal Gupta and Christopher D. Manning. 2015. Distributed representations of words to guide bootstrapped entity classifiers. In *Proceedings of the Conference of the North American Chapter of the Association for Computational Linguistics*.

Himabindu Lakkaraju and Cynthia Rudin. 2016. Learning cost-effective treatment regimes using markov decision processes. *CoRR*, abs/1610.06972.

Omer Levy and Yoav Goldberg. 2014. Dependency-based word embeddings. In *ACL (2)*, pages 302–308.

Laurens van der Maaten and Geoffrey Hinton. 2008. Visualizing data using t-sne. *The Journal of Machine Learning Research*, 9(2579-2605):85.

Tara McIntosh. 2010. Unsupervised discovery of negative categories in lexicon bootstrapping. In *Proceedings of the 2010 Conference on Empirical Methods in Natural Language Processing*, pages 356–365. Association for Computational Linguistics.

Tara McIntosh and James R Curran. 2008. Weighted mutual exclusion bootstrapping for domain independent lexicon and template acquisition. In *Proceedings of the Australasian Language Technology Association Workshop*, volume 2008.

Tomas Mikolov, Ilya Sutskever, Kai Chen, Greg S Corrado, and Jeff Dean. 2013. Distributed representations of words and phrases and their compositionality. In *Advances in neural information processing systems*, pages 3111–3119.

Nikola Mrkšić, Ivan Vulić, Diarmuid Ó Séaghdha, Ira Leviant, Roi Reichart, Milica Gašić, Anna Korhonen, and Steve Young. 2017. Semantic specialization of distributional word vector spaces using monolingual and cross-lingual constraints. *Transactions of the Association for Computational Linguistics*, 5:309–324.

Sameer Pradhan, Alessandro Moschitti, Nianwen Xue, Hwee Tou Ng, Anders Bjrkelund, Olga Uryupina, Yuchen Zhang, and Zhi Zhong. 2013. Towards robust linguistic analysis using ontonotes. In *Proceedings of the Seventeenth Conference on Computational Natural Language Learning*, pages 143–152, Sofia, Bulgaria. Association for Computational Linguistics.

Marco Tulio Ribeiro, Sameer Singh, and Carlos Guestrin. 2016a. "why should i trust you?": Explaining the predictions of any classifier. In *Knowledge Discovery and Data Mining (KDD)*.

Marco Tulio Ribeiro, Sameer Singh, and Carlos Guestrin. 2016b. Why should i trust you?: Explaining the predictions of any classifier. In *Proceedings of the 22nd ACM SIGKDD International Conference on Knowledge Discovery and Data Mining*, pages 1135–1144. ACM.

Marco Tulio Ribeiro, Sameer Singh, and Carlos Guestrin. 2018. Anchors: High-precision model-agnostic explanations. In *AAAI Conference on Artificial Intelligence (AAAI)*.

Sebastian Riedel, Limin Yao, Andrew McCallum, and Benjamin M Marlin. 2013. Relation extraction with matrix factorization and universal schemas. In *Proceedings of NAACL-HLT*.

Ellen Riloff. 1996. Automatically generating extraction patterns from untagged text. In *Proceedings of the national conference on artificial intelligence*, pages 1044–1049.

D. Sculley, Gary Holt, Daniel Golovin, Eugene Davydov, Todd Phillips, Dietmar Ebner, Vinay Chaudhary, and Michael Young. 2014. Machine learning: The high interest credit card of technical debt. In *SE4ML: Software Engineering for Machine Learning (NIPS 2014 Workshop)*.

Rebecca Sharp, Mihai Surdeanu, Peter Jansen, Peter Clark, and Michael Hammond. 2016. Creating causal embeddings for question answering with minimal supervision. In *Proceedings of the Conference on Empirical Methods in Natural Language Processing (EMNLP)*.

Erik F. Tjong Kim Sang and Fien De Meulder. 2003. Introduction to the CoNLL-2003 shared task: Language-independent named entity recognition. In *Proceedings of CoNLL-2003*, pages 142–147. Edmonton, Canada.

Kristina Toutanova, Danqi Chen, Patrick Pantel, Hoifung Poon, Pallavi Choudhury, and Michael Gamon. 2015. Representing text for joint embedding of text and knowledge bases. In *EMNLP*, volume 15, pages 1499–1509. Citeseer.

Kristina Toutanova, Xi Victoria Lin, Wen-tau Yih, Hoifung Poon, and Chris Quirk. 2016. Compositional learning of embeddings for relation paths in knowledge bases and text. In *Proceedings of the 54th Annual Meeting of the Association for Computational Linguistics*, volume 1, pages 1434–1444.

Marco A Valenzuela-Escárcega, Gus Hahn-Powell, Dane Bell, and Mihai Surdeanu. 2016. Snaptogrid: From statistical to interpretable models for biomedical information extraction. In *Proceedings of the 15th Workshop on Biomedical Natural Language Processing*, pages 56–65.

Roman Yangarber. 2003. Counter-training in discovery of semantic patterns. In *Proceedings of the Annual Meeting of the Association for Computational Linguistics*.

David Yarowsky. 1995. Unsupervised word sense disambiguation rivaling supervised methods. In *Proceedings of the Annual Meeting of the Association for Computational Linguistics*.

X. Zhu and Z. Ghahramani. 2002. Learning from labeled and unlabeled data with label propagation. Technical Report CMU-CALD-02-107, Carnegie Mellon University.

Semi-Supervised Teacher-Student Architecture for Relation Extraction

Fan Luo, Ajay Nagesh, Rebecca Sharp, and Mihai Surdeanu
University of Arizona, Tucson, AZ, USA
{fanluo, ajaynagesh, bsharp, msurdeanu}@email.arizona.edu

Abstract

Generating a large amount of training data for information extraction (IE) is either costly (if annotations are created manually), or runs the risk of introducing noisy instances (if distant supervision is used). On the other hand, semi-supervised learning (SSL) is a cost-efficient solution to combat lack of training data. In this paper, we adapt Mean Teacher (Tarvainen and Valpola, 2017), a denoising SSL framework to extract semantic relations between pairs of entities. We explore the sweet spot of amount of supervision required for good performance on this binary relation extraction task. Additionally, different syntax representations are incorporated into our models to enhance the learned representation of sentences. We evaluate our approach on the Google-IISc Distant Supervision (GDS) dataset, which removes test data noise present in all previous distance supervision datasets, which makes it a reliable evaluation benchmark (Jat et al., 2017). Our results show that the SSL Mean Teacher approach nears the performance of fully-supervised approaches even with only 10% of the labeled corpus. Further, the syntax-aware model outperforms other syntax-free approaches across all levels of supervision.

1 Introduction

Occurrences of entities in a sentence are often linked through well-defined relations; e.g., occurrences of PERSON and ORGANIZATION in a sentence may be linked through relations such as *employed at*. The task of relation extraction (RE) is to identify such relations automatically (Pawar et al., 2017). RE is not only crucial for populating knowledge bases with triples consisting of the entity pairs and the extracted relations, but it is also important for any NLP task involving text understanding and inference, such as question answering. In this work, we focus on binary RE, such as identifying the *nationality* relation between two entities, *Kian Tajbakhsh* and *Iran*, in the sentence: *Kian Tajbakhsh is a social scientist who lived for many years in England and the United States before returning to Iran a decade ago.*

Semi-supervised learning (SSL) methods have been shown to work for alleviating the lack of training data in information extraction. For example, bootstrapping learns from a few seed examples and iteratively augments the labeled portion of the data during the training process (Yarowsky, 1995; Collins and Singer, 1999; Carlson et al., 2010; Gupta and Manning, 2015, *inter alia*). However, an important drawback of bootstrapping, which is typically iterative, is that, as learning advances, the task often drifts semantically into a related but different space, e.g., from learning women's names into learning flower names (Yangarber, 2003; McIntosh, 2010). Unlike iterative SSL methods such as bootstrapping, SSL teacher-student networks (Tarvainen and Valpola, 2017; Laine and Aila, 2016; Rasmus et al., 2015) make full use of *both* a small set of labeled examples as well as a large number of unlabeled examples in a one-shot, non-iterative learning process. The unsupervised component uses the unlabeled examples to learn a robust representation of the input data, while the supervised component forces these learned representations to stay relevant to the task.

The contributions of our work are:

(1) We provide a novel application of the Mean Teacher (MT) SSL framework to the task of binary relation extraction. Our approach is simple: we build a student classifier using representation learning of the context between the entity mentions that participate in the given relation. When exposed to unlabeled data, the MT framework learns by maximizing the consistency between a student classifier and a teacher that is an average of

Proceedings of 3rd Workshop on Structured Prediction for NLP, pages 29–37
Minneapolis, Minnesota, June 7, 2019.

past students, where both classifiers are exposed to different noise. For RE, we introduce a strategy to generate noise through word dropout (Iyyer et al., 2015). We provide all code and resources needed to reproduce results[1].

(2) We represent sentences with several types of syntactic abstractions, and employ a simple neural sequence model to embed these representations. We demonstrate in our experiments that the representation that explicitly models syntactic information helps SSL to make the most of limited training data in the RE task.

(3) We evaluate the proposed approach on the Google-IISc Distant Supervision (GDS) dataset introduced in Jat et al. (2017). Our empirical analysis demonstrates that the proposed SSL architecture approaches the performance of state-of-the-art fully-supervised approaches, even when using only 10% of the original labeled corpus.

2 Related work

The exploration of teacher-student models for semi-supervised learning has produced impressive results for image classification (Tarvainen and Valpola, 2017; Laine and Aila, 2016; Rasmus et al., 2015). However, they have not yet been well-studied in the context of natural language processing. Hu et al. (2016) propose a teacher-student model for the task of sentiment classification and named entity recognition, where the teacher is derived from a manually specified set of rule-templates that regularizes a neural student, thereby allowing one to combine neural and symbolic systems. Our MT system is different in that the teacher is a simple running average of the students across different epochs of training, which removes the need of human supervision through rules. More recently, Nagesh and Surdeanu (2018) applied the MT architecture for the task of semi-supervised Named Entity Classification, which is a simpler task compared to our RE task.

Recent works (Liu et al., 2015; Xu et al., 2015; Su et al., 2018) use neural networks to learn syntactic features for relation extraction via traversing the shortest dependency path. Following this trend, we adapt such syntax-based neural models to both of our student and teacher classifiers in the MT architecture.

Both Liu et al. (2015) and Su et al. (2018) use neural networks to encode the words and dependencies along the shortest path between the two entities, and Liu et al. additionally encode the dependency subtrees of the words for additional context. We include this representation (words and dependencies) in our experiments. While the inclusion of the subtrees gives Liu et al. a slight performance boost, here we opt to focus only on the varying representations of the dependency path between the entities, without the additional context.

Su et al. (2018) use an LSTM to model the shortest path between the entities, but keep their lexical and syntactic sequences in separate channels (and they have other channels for additional information such as part of speech (POS)). Rather than maintaining distinct channels for the different representations, here we elect to keep both surface and syntactic forms in the same sequence and instead experiment with different degrees of syntactic representation. We also do not include other types of information (e.g., POS) here, as it is beyond the scope of the current work.

There are several more structured (and more complex) models proposed for relation extraction, e.g., tree-based recurrent neural networks (Socher et al., 2010) and tree LSTMs (Tai et al., 2015). Our semi-supervised framework is an orthogonal improvement, and it is flexible enough to potentially incorporate any of these more complex models.

3 Mean Teacher Framework

Our approach repurposes the Mean Teacher framework for relation extraction. This section an overview of the general MT framework. The next section discusses the adaptation of this framework for RE.

The Mean Teacher (MT) framework, like other teacher-student algorithms, learns from a limited set of labeled data coupled with a much larger corpus of unlabeled data. Intuitively, the larger, unlabeled corpus allows the model to learn a *robust representation* of the input (i.e., one which is not sensitive to noise), and the smaller set of labeled data constrains this learned representation to also be *task-relevant*. This is similar in spirit to an auto-encoder, which learns a representation that is robust to noise in the input. However, auto-encoders generally suffer from a confirmation bias, especially when used in a semi-supervised setting (i.e.,

[1] `https://github.com/Fan-Luo/MT-RelationExtraction`

they tend to overly rely on their own predictions instead of the gold labels (Tarvainen and Valpola, 2017; Laine and Aila, 2016)), providing the motivation for MT. Specifically, to mitigate confirmation bias, and regularize the model, the teacher weights in MT are not directly learned, but rather they are an *average* of the learned student weights, similar in spirit to the averaged perceptron. This provides a more robust scaffolding that the student model can rely on during training when gold labels are unavailable (Nagesh and Surdeanu, 2018).

The MT architecture is summarized in Figure 1. It consists of two models, *teacher* and *student*, both with identical architectures (but different weights). While the weights for the student model are learned through standard backpropagation, the weights in the teacher network are set through an exponential moving average of the student weights. The same data point, augmented with noise (see Section 4.2), is input to both the teacher and the student models.

The MT algorithm is designed for semi-supervised tasks, where only a few of the data points are labeled in training. The cost function is a linear combination of two different type of costs: *classification* and *consistency*. The classification cost applies to labeled data points, and can be instantiated with any standard supervised cost function (e.g., we used categorical cross-entropy, which is based on the softmax over the label categories). The consistency cost is used for unlabeled data points, and aims to minimize the differences in predictions between the teacher and the student models. The consistency cost, J is:

$$J(\theta) = \mathrm{E}_{x,\eta',\eta}\left[\|f(x,\theta',\eta') - f(x,\theta,\eta)\|^2\right] \quad (1)$$

where, given an input x, this function is defined as the expected distance between the prediction of the student model ($f(x,\theta,\eta)$, with weights θ and noise η) and the prediction of the teacher model ($f(x,\theta',\eta')$ with weights θ' and noise η'). Here, our predictions are the models' output distributions (with a softmax) across all labels.

Importantly, as hinted above, only the student model is updated via backpropagation. On the other hand, the gradients are not backpropagated through the teacher weights, rather they are deterministically updated after each mini-batch of gradient descent in the student. The update uses an exponentially-weighted moving average (EMA) that combines the previous teacher with the latest version of the student:

$$\theta'_t = \alpha\theta'_{t-1} + (1-\alpha)\theta_t \quad (2)$$

where θ'_t is defined at training step t as the EMA of successive weights θ. This averaging strategy is reminiscent of the average perceptron, except in this case the average is not constructed through an error-driven algorithm, but, instead, it is controlled by a hyper parameter α.

4 Task-specific Representation

The MT framework contains two components that are task specific. The first is the representation of the input to be modeled, which consists of entity mention pairs and the context between the two entity mentions. The second is the strategy for inserting noise in the inputs received by the student and teacher models. We detail both these components here.

4.1 Input Representations

Within the Mean Teacher framework, we investigate input representations of four types of syntactic abstraction. Each corresponds to one of the inputs shown in Figure 2 for the example (*Robert Kingsley*, `perGraduatedInstitution`, *University of Minnesota*).

Average: Our shallowest learned representation uses the surface form of the entities (e.g., *Robert Kingsley* and *University of Minnesota*) and the context between them. If there are several mentions of one or both of the entities in a given sentence, we used the closest pair. The model averages the word embeddings for all tokens and then passes it through a fully-connected feed-forward neural network, with one hidden layer and finally to an output layer for classification into the the relation labels.

Surface LSTM (surfaceLSTM): The next learned representation also uses the surface form of the input, i.e., the sequence of words between the two entities, but replaces the word embedding average with a single-layer bidirectional LSTM, which have been demonstrated to encode some syntactic information (Peters et al., 2018). The representation from the LSTM is passed to the feed-forward network as above.

Head LSTM (headLSTM): Under the intuition that the trigger is the most important lexical item in the context of a relation, relation extraction

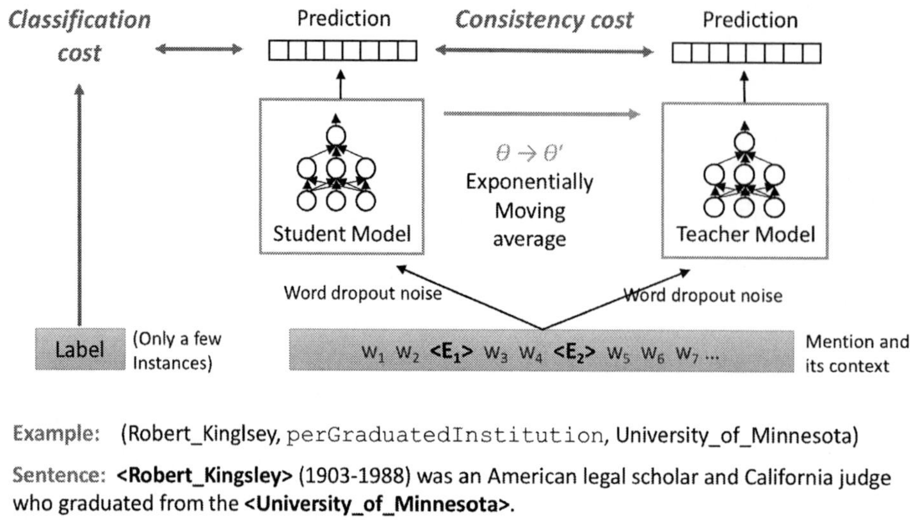

Figure 1: The Mean Teacher (MT) framework for relation extraction which makes use of a large, unlabeled corpus and a small number of labeled data points. Intuitively, the larger, unlabeled corpus allows the model to learn a *robust representation* of the input (i.e., one which is not sensitive to noise), and the smaller set of labeled data constrains this learned representation to also be *task-relevant*. Here, for illustration, we depict the training step with one labeled example. The MT framework consists of two models: a *student model* which is trained through backpropagation, and a *teacher model* which is not directly trained, but rather is an average of previous student models (i.e., its weights are updated through an exponential moving average of the student weights at each epoch). Each model takes the same input, but augmented with different noise (here, word dropout). The inputs consist of (a) a pair of entity mentions (here, $\langle E_1 \rangle$: *Robert_Kingsley* and $\langle E_2 \rangle$: *University_of_Minnesota*), and (b) the context in which they occur (i.e., *(1903-1988) was an American legal scholar and California judge who graduated from the*). Each model produces a prediction for the label of the data point (i.e., a distribution over the classes). There are two distinct costs in the MT framework: the *consistency cost* and the *classification cost*. The consistency cost constrains the output label distribution of the two models to be the similar, and it is applied to both labeled and unlabeled inputs (as these distributions can be constrained even if the true label is unknown) to ensure that the learned representations (distributions) are not sensitive to the applied noise. When the model is given a labeled input, it additionally assigns a classification cost using the prediction of the student model. This guides the learned representation to be useful to the task at hand.

can often be distilled into the task of identifying and classifying *triggers*, i.e., words which signal specific relations (Yu and Ji, 2016). For example, the verb *died* is highly indicative of the `placeOfDeath` relation. There are several ways of finding a candidate trigger such as the PageRank-inspired approach of Yu and Ji (2016). Here, for simplicity, we use the governing head of the two entities within their token interval (i.e., the node in the dependency graph that dominates the two entities) as a proxy for the trigger. We then create the shortest dependency paths from it to each of the two entities, and concatenate these two sequences to form the representation of the corresponding relation mention. This is shown as the head-lexicalized syntactic path in Figure 2. For this representation, we once again pass this token sequence to the LSTM and subsequent feed-forward network.

Syntactic LSTM (synLSTM): Compared with headLSTM, our syntactic LSTM traverses the directed shortest path between the two entities through the dependency syntax graph for the sentence, instead of concatenated shortest dependency paths between the trigger and each entity. As shown in the fully lexicalized syntactic path in Figure 2, we include in the representation the directed dependencies traversed (e.g., `<nsubj` for an incoming `nsubj` dependency), as well as all the words along the path (i.e., *scholar* and *graduated*)[2]. We feed these tokens, both words and dependencies, to the same LSTM as above.

4.2 Noise Regularization

One critical component of the Mean Teacher framework is the addition of independent noise to both the student and the teacher models (Laine

[2]For multi-sentence instances where no single sentence contains both entities, in order to obtain a syntactic parse, we concatenate the closest sentences with each of the entities with a semi-colon and use that as our sentence. While this could be resolved more cleanly with discourse information or cross-sentence dependencies, that is beyond the scope of the current work.

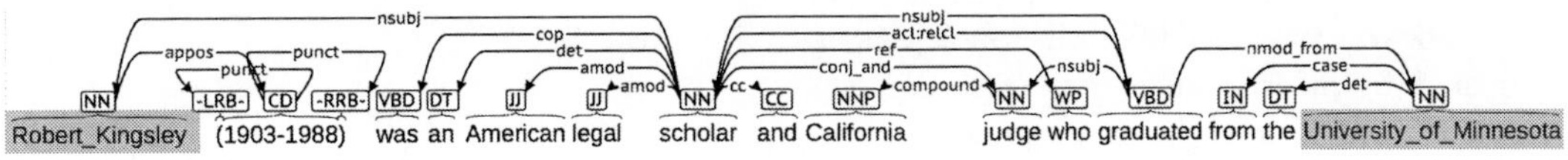

Surface: Robert_Kingsley (1903-1988) was an American legal scholar and California judge who graduated from the University_of_Minnesota

Surface Syntactic Path: Robert_ Kingsley scholar graduated University_of_Minnesota

Head Lexicalized Syntactic Path: Robert_Kingsley <nsubj scholar >acl:relcl >nmod_from University_of_Minnesota

Fully Lexicalized Syntactic Path: Robert_Kingsley <nsubj scholar >acl:relcl graduated >nmod_from University_of_Minnesota

Figure 2: Examples of the varying degrees of syntactic structure used for our models. The *surface* representation consists of a bag of entities (shown in blue) and the words that come between them. The *surface syntactic path* includes the words along the shortest path between the entities. The *head lexicalized syntactic* representation contains the governing head of the structure that dominates the two entities, and the directed dependencies connecting it to each of the entities. The *fully lexicalized syntactic* representation contains the directed dependencies along the shortest path in addition to the words along the shortest path. For both *head lexicalized syntactic* and *fully lexicalized syntactic* representation, the dependency notations include the dependency labels as well as the direction of the dependency arc ($<$: right-to-left, $>$: left-to-right). Both words and syntactic dependencies are converted to embeddings that are trained along with the rest of the model.

and Aila, 2016; Tarvainen and Valpola, 2017). While in some tasks, e.g., image classification, Gaussian noise is added to the network (Rasmus et al., 2015), here we opted to follow the example of Iyyer et al. (2015) and Nagesh and Surdeanu (2018) and use word dropout for the needed noise. For each training instance we randomly drop k tokens from the input sequence.[3] The random dropout for the student model is independent from that of the teacher model, in principle forcing the learned representations to be robust to noise and learn noise-invariant abstract latent representations for the task.

5 Experiments

5.1 Data

We evaluate our approach on **Google-IISc Distant Supervision (GDS) dataset**. This is a distant supervision dataset introduced by Jat et al. (2017) that aligns the Google Relation Extraction Corpus[4] with texts retrieved through web search. Importantly, the dataset was curated to ensure that at least one sentence for a given entity pair supports the corresponding relation between the entities. It contains five relations including *NA*. The training partition contains 11,297 instances (2,772 are NA), the development partition contains 1,864 instances (447 NA), and the test partition contains 5663 instances (1360 NA). The dataset is divided such that there is no overlap among entity pairs between these partitions.

5.2 Semi-Supervised Setup

In order to examine the utility of our semi-supervised approach, we evaluate our approach with different levels of supervision by artificially manipulating the fully-labeled datasets described in Section 5.1 to contain varying amounts of unlabeled instances. To do this, we incrementally selected random portions of the training data to serve as labeled data, the rest being treated as unlabeled data (i.e., their labels are masked to not be visible to the classifier). In other words, this unlabeled data was used to calculate the *consistency cost*, but not the *classification cost*. We experimented with using 1%, 10%, 50%, and 100% of the labeled training data for supervision.

5.3 Baselines

Previous work: We compare our model against the previous state-of-the-art work in Jat et al. (2017). They propose two *fully-supervised* models: a bidirectional gated recurrent unit neural network with word attention (their BGWA model) and a piecewise convolutional neural network (PCNN) with an entity attention layer (their EA model), which is itself based on the PCNN approach of Zeng et al. (2015). Since we use single models only, we omit Jat et al.'s supervised ensemble for a more direct comparison. Note these two approaches are state-of-the-art methods for RE that rely on more complex attention-based models. On the other hand, in this work we use only vanilla LSTMs for both of our student and teacher models. However, since the MT framework is agnostic to the student model, in fu-

[3]In this work we use $k = 1$. In initial experiments, other values of k did not change results significantly.

[4]https://research.googleblog.com/2013/04/50000-lessons-on-how-to-read-relation.html

ture work we can potentially further increase performance by incorporating these more complex methods in our semi-supervised approach.

Student Only: In order to determine the contribution of the Mean Teacher framework itself, in each setting (amount of supervision and input representation) we additionally compare against a baseline consisting of our student model trained without the teacher (i.e., we remove the consistency cost component from the cost function).

5.4 Model Tuning

We lightly tuned the approach and hyperparameters on the development partitions. We built our architecture in PyTorch[5], a popular deep learning library, extending the framework of Tarvainen and Valpola (2017)[6]. For our model, we used a bidirectional LSTM with a hidden size of 50. The subsequent fully connected network has one hidden layer of 100 dimensions and *ReLU* activations. The training was done with the Adam optimizer (Kingma and Ba, 2015) with the default learning rate (0.1). We initialized our word embeddings with GloVe 100-dimensional embeddings (Pennington et al., 2014)[7]. The dependency embeddings were also of size 100 and were randomly initialized. Both of these embedding were allowed to update during training. Any word or token which occurred fewer than 5 times in a dataset was treated as unknown. For our word dropout, we removed one word from each input at random. MT has some additional parameters: the *consistency cost weight* (the weight given to the consistency component of the cost function) and the *EMA decay rate* (α in Eq. 2). We set these to be 1.0 and 0.99 respectively. Akin to a burn-in at the beginning of training, we had an initial consistency cost weight of 0.0 and allowed it to ramp up to the full value over the coarse of training using a *consistency ramp up* of 5.

During training, we saved model checkpoints every 10 epochs, and ran our models up to a maximum of 200 epochs. We chose the best model by tracking the teacher performance on the development partition and using the model checkpoint immediately following the maximum performance.

[5]https://pytorch.org

[6]https://github.com/CuriousAI/mean-teacher

[7]https://nlp.stanford.edu/projects/glove

6 Results

We evaluate our approach on the GDS dataset, across the various levels of supervision detailed in Section 5. The precision, recall, and F1 scores are provided in Table 1.

In the evaluation, we consider only the top label assigned by the model, counting it as a match only if (a) it matches the correct label and (b) the label is not NA. For each setting, we provide the final performance of both the student network and the teacher network. We also compare against the baseline student network (i.e., the network trained without the consistency cost).

In Table 1 we see that in general the MT framework improves performance over the student-only baseline, with the sole exception of when there is only 1% supervision. The large performance gap between the 1% and 10% supervision configurations for the student-only model indicates that 1% supervision provides an inadequate amount of labeled data to support learning the different relation types. Further, when the unlabeled data overwhelms the supervised data, the MT framework encourages the student model to drift away from the correct labels through the consistence cost. Therefore, in this situation with insufficient supervision, the student-only approach performs better than MT. This result highlights the importance of a balance between the supervised and unsupervised training partitions within the MT framework.

Among our MT models, we see that while the surfaceLSTM models perform better than the Average models, the models which explicitly represent the syntactic dependency path between the entities have the strongest performance. This is true for both the student-only as well as the MT framework. In particular, we find that the best performing model is the synLSTM. These results show that: (a) while surface LSTMs may loosely model syntax (Linzen et al., 2016), they are still largely complemented by syntax-based representation, and, more importantly, (b) syntax provides improved generalization power over surface information.

6.1 Comparison to Prior Work

We additionally compare our Mean Teacher synLSTM model, against the BGWA and EA models of Jat et al. (2017). For an accurate comparison, here we follow their setup closely. For each entity pair that occurs in test, we aggregate

Model		100% Prec / Recall / F1	50% Prec / Recall / F1	10% Prec / Recall / F1	1% Prec / Recall / F1
Student-Only Baseline					
Average	Student	0.724 / 0.793 / 0.757±0.00	0.716 / 0.774 / 0.744±0.01	0.718 / 0.684 / 0.700±0.01	0.624 / 0.572 / 0.597±0.01
surfaceLSTM	Student	0.754 / 0.830 / 0.790±0.01	0.748 / 0.834 / 0.788±0.01	0.735 / 0.752 / 0.744±0.00	0.691 / 0.622 / 0.655±0.01
headLSTM	Student	0.739 / 0.808 / 0.772±0.01	0.725 / 0.816 / 0.767±0.00	0.697 / 0.723 / 0.709±0.01	0.633 / 0.630 / 0.631±0.01
synLSTM	Student	0.757 / 0.828 / 0.791±0.00	0.759 / 0.827 / 0.791±0.00	0.716 / 0.770 / 0.742±0.01	0.667 / 0.677 / **0.671±0.01**
Mean Teacher Framework					
Average	Student	0.719 / 0.717 / 0.716±0.04	0.739 / 0.718 / 0.728±0.01	0.715 / 0.645 / 0.677±0.02	0.611 / 0.509 / 0.555±0.02
	Teacher	0.733 / 0.767 / 0.750±0.00	0.724 / 0.747 / 0.735±0.00	0.718 / 0.649 / 0.682±0.01	0.611 / 0.503 / 0.552±0.01
surfaceLSTM	Student	0.760 / 0.745 / 0.752±0.01	0.762 / 0.792 / 0.777±0.00	0.725 / 0.712 / 0.718±0.00	0.546 / 0.440 / 0.486±0.07
	Teacher	0.761 / 0.819 / 0.789±0.00	0.760 / 0.817 / 0.787±0.00	0.735 / 0.733 / 0.734±0.01	0.538 / 0.438 / 0.482±0.06
headLSTM	Student	0.718 / 0.766 / 0.741±0.01	0.728 / 0.786 / 0.756±0.01	0.700 / 0.684 / 0.692±0.01	0.613 / 0.525 / 0.565±0.00
	Teacher	0.728 / 0.815 / 0.769±0.00	0.731 / 0.800 / 0.764±0.00	0.703 / 0.717 / 0.710±0.01	0.611 / 0.527 / 0.566±0.01
synLSTM	Student	0.753 / 0.780 / 0.766±0.01	0.751 / 0.826 / 0.786±0.01	0.724 / 0.732 / 0.728±0.01	0.634 / 0.590 / 0.609±0.03
	Teacher	0.764 / 0.846 / **0.803±0.00**	0.763 / 0.833 / **0.796±0.00**	0.734 / 0.759 / **0.746±0.00**	0.632 / 0.574 / 0.601±0.03

Table 1: Performance on the GDS dataset for our baseline models (i.e, student-only without the Mean Teacher framework) and for our Mean Teacher models (both the student and teacher performance is provided). We report precision, recall, and F1 score for each of the input representations (Average, surfaceLSTM, headLSTM, and synLSTM), with varying proportions of training labels (100%, 50%, 10% and 1% of the training data labeled). Each value is the average of three runs with different random seed initializations, and for the F1 scores we additionally provide the standard deviation across the different runs.

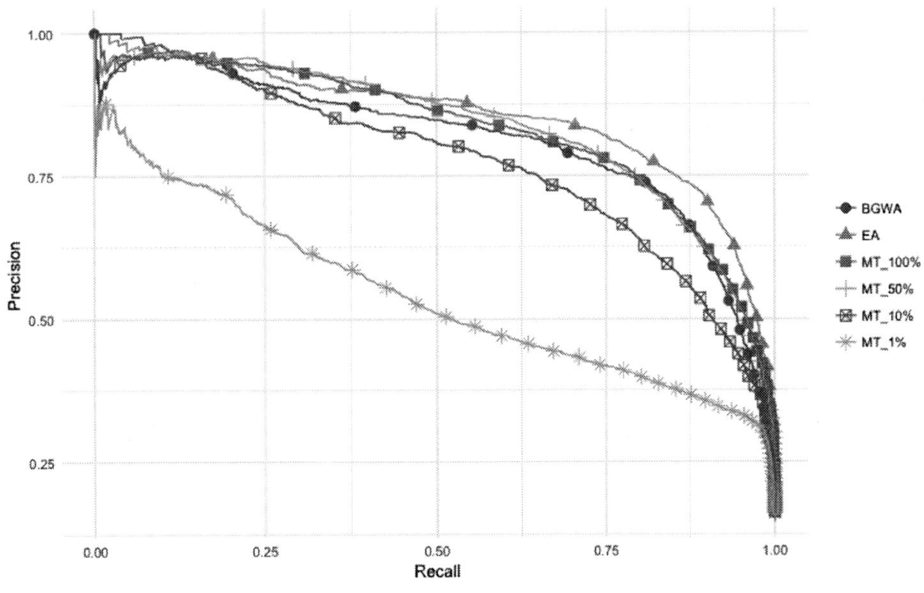

Figure 3: Precision-recall curves for the GDS dataset. We include two prior systems (BGWA and EA) as well as our Mean Teacher approach using our best performing input representation (synLSTM) for increasing amounts of supervision (from 1% of the training labels to 100%, or fully supervised).

the model's predictions for all mentions of that entity pair using the Noisy-Or formula into a single distribution for our model across *all* labels, except for NA, and plot the precision-recall (PR) curve accordingly.

Data for the BGWA and EA models was taken from author-provided results files[8], allowing us to plot additional values beyond what was previously published. The PR curves for each level of supervision are shown in Figures 3.

We observe that our fully supervised model performs very similarly to the fully-supervised model of Jat et al. (2017). This is encouraging, considering that our approach is simpler, e.g., we do not have an attention model. Critically, we see that under the Mean Teacher framework, this pattern continues even as we decrease the amount of supervision such that even with only 10% of the original training data we approach their fully-supervised performance. It is not until we use two orders of magnitude fewer labeled examples that we see a major degradation in performance. This demonstrates the utility of our syntax-aware MT approach for learning robust representations for relation extraction.

7 Conclusion

This paper introduced a neural model for semi-supervised relation extraction. Our syntactically-informed, semi-supervised approach learns effectively to extract a number of relations from very limited labeled training data by employing a Mean Teacher (MT) architecture. This framework combines a student trained through backpropagation with a teacher that is an average of past students. Each model is exposed to different noise, which we created in this work through word dropout. The approach uses unlabeled data through a consistency cost, which encourages the student to stay close to the predictions of the teacher, and labeled data, through a standard classification cost. The consistency requirement between the student and the teacher ensures that the learned representation of the input is robust to noise, while the classification requirement ensures that this learned representation encodes the task-specific information necessary to correctly extract relations between entities.

We empirically demonstrated that our approach is able to perform close to more complex, fully-supervised approaches using only 10% of the training data for relation extraction. This work further supports our previous work on MT for the task of named entity classification, where we observed similar gains (Nagesh and Surdeanu, 2018). Further, we show that the MT framework performs reliably for various input representations (from purely surface forms all the way to primarily syntactic). We additionally demonstrate that explicitly representing syntax, even in simplified ways, is beneficial to the models across all levels of supervision.

[8]https://github.com/SharmisthaJat/RE-DS-Word-Attention-Models

8 Acknowledgments

This work was supported by the Defense Advanced Research Projects Agency (DARPA) under the World Modelers program, grant number W911NF1810014, and by the Bill and Melinda Gates Foundation HBGDki Initiative. Mihai Surdeanu declares a financial interest in lum.ai. This interest has been properly disclosed to the University of Arizona Institutional Review Committee and is managed in accordance with its conflict of interest policies.

References

Andrew Carlson, Justin Betteridge, Bryan Kisiel, Burr Settles, Estevam R. Hruschka Jr., and Tom M. Mitchell. 2010. Toward an architecture for never-ending language learning. In *Proc. of AAAI*.

Michael Collins and Yoram Singer. 1999. Unsupervised models for named entity classification. In *Proc. of EMNLP*.

Sonal Gupta and Christopher D. Manning. 2015. Distributed representations of words to guide bootstrapped entity classifiers. In *Proc. of NAACL*.

Zhiting Hu, Xuezhe Ma, Zhengzhong Liu, Eduard Hovy, and Eric Xing. 2016. Harnessing deep neural networks with logic rules. *arXiv preprint arXiv:1603.06318*.

Mohit Iyyer, Varun Manjunatha, Jordan Boyd-Graber, and Hal Daumé III. 2015. Deep unordered composition rivals syntactic methods for text classification. In *Proc. of ACL-IJCNLP*, volume 1, pages 1681–1691.

Sharmistha Jat, Siddhesh Khandelwal, and Partha Talukdar. 2017. Improving distantly supervised relation extraction using word and entity based attention. In *Proc. of AKBC*.

Diederik P. Kingma and Jimmy Ba. 2015. Adam: A method for stochastic optimization. In *Proceedings of the 3rd International Conference on Learning Representations (ICLR)*.

Samuli Laine and Timo Aila. 2016. Temporal ensembling for semi-supervised learning. *CoRR*, abs/1610.02242.

Tal Linzen, Emmanuel Dupoux, and Yoav Goldberg. 2016. Assessing the ability of lstms to learn syntax-sensitive dependencies. *Transactions of the Association for Computational Linguistics*, 4:521–535.

Yang Liu, Furu Wei, Sujian Li, Heng Ji, Ming Zhou, and Houfeng WANG. 2015. A dependency-based neural network for relation classification. In *Proc. of ACL-IJCNLP*, pages 285–290, Beijing, China.

Tara McIntosh. 2010. Unsupervised discovery of negative categories in lexicon bootstrapping. In *Proceedings of the 2010 Conference on Empirical Methods in Natural Language Processing*, pages 356–365.

Ajay Nagesh and Mihai Surdeanu. 2018. An exploration of three lightly-supervised representation learning approaches for named entity classification. In *Proceedings of the 27th International Conference on Computational Linguistics*, pages 2312–2324.

Sachin Pawar, Girish K. Palshikar, and Pushpak Bhattacharyya. 2017. Relation extraction : A survey.

Jeffrey Pennington, Richard Socher, and Christopher D. Manning. 2014. Glove: Global vectors for word representation. In *EMNLP*, pages 1532–1543.

Matthew Peters, Mark Neumann, Mohit Iyyer, Matt Gardner, Christopher Clark, Kenton Lee, and Luke Zettlemoyer. 2018. Deep contextualized word representations. In *Proc. of NAACL*, pages 2227–2237.

Antti Rasmus, Mathias Berglund, Mikko Honkala, Harri Valpola, and Tapani Raiko. 2015. Semi-supervised learning with ladder networks. In C. Cortes, N. D. Lawrence, D. D. Lee, M. Sugiyama, and R. Garnett, editors, *Proc. of NIPS*, pages 3546–3554. Curran Associates, Inc.

Richard Socher, Christopher D Manning, and Andrew Y Ng. 2010. Learning continuous phrase representations and syntactic parsing with recursive neural networks. In *Proceedings of the NIPS-2010 Deep Learning and Unsupervised Feature Learning Workshop*, volume 2010, pages 1–9.

Yu Su, Honglei Liu, Semih Yavuz, Izzeddin Gur, Huan Sun, and Xifeng Yan. 2018. Global relation embedding for relation extraction. In *Proc. of NAACL-HLT*, pages 820–830, New Orleans, Louisiana.

Kai Sheng Tai, Richard Socher, and Christopher D Manning. 2015. Improved semantic representations from tree-structured long short-term memory networks. *arXiv preprint arXiv:1503.00075*.

Antti Tarvainen and Harri Valpola. 2017. Mean teachers are better role models: Weight-averaged consistency targets improve semi-supervised deep learning results. In *Advances in neural information processing systems*, pages 1195–1204.

Yan Xu, Lili Mou, Ge Li, Yunchuan Chen, Hao Peng, and Zhi Jin. 2015. Classifying relations via long short term memory networks along shortest dependency paths. In *Proc. of EMNLP*, pages 1785–1794.

Roman Yangarber. 2003. Counter-training in discovery of semantic patterns. In *Proc. of ACL*.

David Yarowsky. 1995. Unsupervised word sense disambiguation rivaling supervised methods. In *Proc. of ACL*.

Dian Yu and Heng Ji. 2016. Unsupervised person slot filling based on graph mining. In *Proc. of ACL*, volume 1, pages 44–53.

Daojian Zeng, Kang Liu, Yubo Chen, and Jun Zhao. 2015. Distant supervision for relation extraction via piecewise convolutional neural networks. In *EMNLP*.

Author Index

Association for Computational Linguistics
209 N. Eighth Street
Stroudsburg, Pennsylvania 18360

ISBN 978-1-5108-8769-5

9 781510 887695

CURRAN ASSOCIATES INC.
proceedings.com